THE STRATEGY QUEST

THE STRATEGY QUEST

Releasing the Energy of Manufacturing
within a
Market Driven Strategy

"A Dynamic Business Story"

TERRY HILL

AMD PUBLISHING (uk)

AMD Publishing (UK)
16, Collett Walk, Windmill Fields, Coventry CV1 4PT

Published by AMD Publishing (UK), 1998
First published in Great Britain 1994 by Pitman Publishing

The figure reproduced on page 35 is taken from *Manufacturing Strategy, Text and Cases,*
2nd edition, p 18, Terry Hill, Irwin 1994, with permisssion

3 5 7 9 10 8 6 4 2

Photoset in Linotron Times

ISBN 1 869937 01 5

Printed and bound in Great Britain by
J W Arrowsmith Limited
Bristol

CONTENTS

FOREWORD

In many firms, corporate strategy is developed as a series of independent statements. Lacking essential integration, the result is a compilation of distinct, functional strategies which sit side by side, layer on layer in the same corporate binder. Integration is not provided if, in fact, it was ever intended. Hence, many functional strategies are characterised by their reactive nature rather than their being an essential part of the corporate debate leading to agreed strategic direction. Without this, companies ignore that just as markets have an internal dimension in that they place demands within a company, manufacturing has an external dimension in terms of its ability to support the needs of chosen markets.

This problem is made worse when companies seek to resolve strategic approaches by reviewing companies as wholes, typically undertaken by overlaying corporate diversity with generic, strategic solutions. Niche, low cost, core competence-type arguments are seductive in their apparent offerings. The promise of uniformity is appealing to those with the task of developing strategies for businesses which are typified by difference not similarity. In fact, such approaches purport to identify a corporate similarity which, though desirable, is inherently not available. The alternative is to recognise difference and develop multi-strategies to address these separate needs.

Strategy problems are complex. To resolve them a company needs first, concepts to give insights and to help choose between outcomes, second, a recognition that it is a problem requiring an intellectual resolution and, third, a willingness to work hard. And, that's a difficult trio. For strategy is not a process leading to generalisations. Nothing would be further from the truth. It's a distillation process with the task of identifying the very essence of what comprises a business.

These sets of complex issues are bound together both in their source and solution. Hopefully, the uncertainty and iterative nature of the strategic debates which characterise successful outcomes are provided by this book. Though unusual in its format you will find its origins are commonplace.

Chapter 1

"Sales are up,
but not profits"

The alarm went off as it always did at 5:45. John Hart rolled over and stretched out an arm to stifle its beeping. He lay still in the darkness, listening to the wind outside and subconsciously bracing himself for the day.

It came to him slowly that he was alone in the bed, and then he remembered that Wendy had spent the previous night in Toronto. She always stayed in the city when she had gallery openings; she was seldom finished before two in the morning, and it was forty miles door to door. A room at the University Women's Club made more sense.

Hart hoped she was sleeping in this morning, but rather doubted it. He stretched out his arm again, and turned on the light.

Downstairs he ate a bowl of cereal and listened to the six-o'clock news on CBC, while the wind continued to whistle through the trees in the yard. He shaved and dressed meticulously. One day, when the feeling of being the new kid on the block had dissipated, he might revert to shirt sleeves and slacks like some of his colleagues, but for the moment it was still shirt and tie. Wendy, who always dressed impeccably for the office, sometimes teased him about this, saying he was the best-dressed manufacturing executive in south-western Ontario.

It was 6:20. He opened his briefcase, checked the papers inside and snapped it shut. Out in the garage it was chilly, dark and damp; a typical March morning. He climbed in behind the wheel of his Ford Bronco and turned the key. Warming the engine for a moment, he pressed the button on the garage door opener, turned on the lights and drove into the yard.

The lane leading towards the road was half a mile long and, at this time of the year, thick with slush and mud. Hart was English, and had lived the first thirty-five years of his life in that country; he liked small cars, and was still finding the Bronco hard to get used to. But you couldn't live out here in the winter without four-wheel drive, not if you wanted to get to work every morning. It was a small price to pay for the peace and quiet of their crumbling old farmhouse. They had been in the house for six months now, moving out from Mississauga, and nothing on earth could have drawn Hart back.

The house was, in fact, a result of his new job. He had been tipped about the promotion a year ago, and indeed he had been aware for some time that Laurentian, the parent group, was grooming him for a chief executive officer's job. Laurentian was an American-based corporation involved in engineering, fabrication and packaging in the United States, Canada and Europe.

Hart had been a highly successful manufacturing director, first with an engineering firm in Toronto and then for an Oshawa auto parts maker, both part of the Laurentian empire. After the second job, they sent him off to be finance director of a Burlington firm, to 'broaden his horizons,' as the group vice-president put it, and then in July, they had told him they were going to give him his own company: Wentworth Mouldings in Hamilton. With Wendy's business also expanding steadily westward from Toronto, it made sense to move out. They bought the farmhouse in July and moved in August. Suddenly, it seemed he was getting everything he wanted.

That had been last year. He had taken over at Wentworth in September, with great plans for growing the company and making his mark. He was aware Wentworth had problems, though not serious ones; the company seemed to be losing its way and performance was dropping below Group targets, for no apparent reason. Martin Kirk, the previous CEO, had been a competent enough man, but he had sensed the need for change for both himself and for Wentworth and had asked Laurentian to move him on. Hart was sure that his new blood was all that was needed to get Wentworth back on track.

It hadn't quite worked out that way. It was now March, and he had made no real progress. He could feel the pressure building.

He reached the end of the lane and shifted out of four wheel drive, turning onto the paved road that led down across Highway 5 to the Queen Elizabeth Way. He had a busy day – in fact, a busy week – ahead of him. The morning tour of the factory and an afternoon board meeting were going to chew up the day. Much of the rest of it, he knew from experience, would disappear in meetings, phone calls and answering letters. Somewhere, somehow, he was going to have to make time to start studying the problems Wentworth faced. As a first step, he was going to bring up the issue at the board meeting this afternoon and ask his directors and senior managers a simple question: where was Wentworth going?

He knew he was expected to lead and that it was up to him to provide, as well as elicit, insights and then drive decisions through. At the same time, his senior executives knew the company better than he did, and all would have their own role to play in any future strategy for Wentworth; whatever that strategy might turn out to be. He resolved to work harder at team-building and to make sure his top managers functioned more as a unit, rather than as department heads fighting in their own corners.

Then there was the problem of investment. Three weeks earlier he had written to the Group spelling out his plans for expansion of production facilities and asking Laurentian to provide investment capital. He didn't think, in retrospect, that he had put his case very well, and some of his explanations about the need for growth and desire to develop markets more fully had sounded unconvincing, even to him. But surely the logic of the situation – that Wentworth, which was already running at full throttle, needed more production capacity – was obvious. Both his marketing and manufacturing directors concurred that new investment was vital to the growing company. Surely Laurentian would give him the money he needed, and that would be a giant step forward.

If they didn't, it was possible that Wentworth would continue to stagnate. He pulled the Bronco out to pass a slow-moving truck, its running lights piercing the pre-dawn haze, and swung back in again, seeing the sodium lights of the QEW up ahead. What was Wentworth's problem? he wondered, not for the first time. Full order books, production running on three shifts, and yet they seemed to be bumping their heads on a ceiling, a limit to growth which some force had conspired to impose upon them. The only way forward he could see was to expand the factory, produce more, acquire more and bigger orders from more and bigger customers. And to do that, he needed investment.

Hart pulled onto the Queen Elizabeth Way, swung into the middle lane and turned on the radio. The sports news was on; the Maple Leafs had won in New York. He smiled wryly. There would be celebrations at the plant; in a country where hockey was already a national fixation, the employees at Wentworth were more than usually obsessed.

Then the business news. He listened out of habit to what was already happening on the London markets. Looking out the window as he drove southwest past the suburbs of Burlington, he saw the first light growing in the sky. The weather was clear and windy, but not as cold as it had been. There had been two inches of snow on Monday, and the materials delivery had been four hours late. Traffic was growing heavy as he drove past Hamilton Harbour and turned off onto Centennial Parkway. Another twenty minutes and he was pulling through the gates and into the factory's gravel yard.

The office block was a low white building set in front of a long shed where the moulding machines were working. He could hear the extraction fans humming, and wisps of steam were rising in the cold. More cars were pulling in behind him, the day shift getting ready for work. Dave Kochner, one of the day-shift supervisors, got out of his pickup truck and waved. 'Morning, Mr. Hart!'

'Morning, Dave. Who won the pool on the hockey game?'

'Donnie Newton on the night shift. Good game, boss, did you see it?'

Hart smiled and shook his head. Eight years in Canada had not been enough to make a hockey fan out of John Hart, but he did his best to hide it. Kochner went off toward the staff cateferia on the far side of the yard. A few other men passed and waved, and Hart saw Judy Salucci, one of the receptionists, pull up in her rusty old car, peering through holes she had scraped in the thick frost on her windshield. 'Morning, Judy. You're here bright and early.'

'I have some typing to do,' said Judy. She was muffled up to the chin, and Hart suspected her car heater didn't work. He knew she drove from the far side of Hamilton, and he made a mental note to find out from Tim Pringle, the personnel manager, what her salary was and whether the firm could help her with an auto loan.

In reception, Hart smelled coffee in the air. His secretary, Darlene Myers, always came in early, unasked, on board-meeting mornings. Hart appreciated the effort. Most days he came alone into the office, made his own coffee, sorted his mail and had a clear hour to himself before the rest of the office staff arrived at 8:30. However, Darlene had a tendency to tiptoe around him when she suspected he was trying to think, which proved distracting, but a small price to pay.

'Good morning, John. Coffee's ready, and I've sorted the mail.'

'Thanks. Darlene. You know, you really don't have to come in early just because there's a board meeting.'

'I know, but I like to be on hand in case there's anything I can do. Something might come up at the last minute.'

Hart poured a cup of coffee and looked through the mountain of mail – a trade magazine, which he would probably never have time to read; a questionnaire from a research company, ditto. In theory Hart was all in favour of business research, but in practice, he simply didn't have time to participate. He read the first paragraph of a letter from Conway Foods, a customer, and then initialled it for the attention of Tony Leclerc, the marketing director. The remainder could comfortably rest in his in-box for awhile. At the bottom of the stack sat a single-page letter on cream stationery with Laurentian letterhead from the head office in Philadelphia.

Dear John,

I feel I ought to apologize on behalf of the board of directors for taking so long to respond to your capital expenditure proposal. In fact, we have looked over the details with a great deal of interest, and in theory, we see no reason why you shouldn't expand Wentworth Mouldings' production capacity.

However, I also have to tell you that we have certain reservations. We have felt for some time that Wentworth was not performing up to par. As you pointed out, sales have been increasing. However, as you also pointed out, quite frankly, profits have definitely plateaued. I don't want to sound like a miser, but there's a general feeling that we need to see what can be done about improving Wentworth's profit position before we put money into expanding production. We want to make sure we get a bang for our buck.

Just so that you are clear on this, I want you to realise that we are not turning you down out of hand, and we are interested in seeing Wentworth grow. Come up with a strategy that tells us how you propose to manage that growth, and we'll be right behind you; but not, I'm afraid, before then.

Sorry not to be more positive about this. Good luck with sorting things out.

Best wishes,

Mike Connors
Vice-President, Industrial Division

He sipped his coffee, staring out at the courtyard where the morning light was glinting off slushy pools. In other words, Group was saying, 'nice try.'

So much for a flying start this morning. After that, nothing seemed to go according to plan. His hour for contemplation vanished all too soon. He was barely at his desk when the phone rang. Darlene told him the CEO of Conway Foods was on the line, wanting to speak to him. After 20 minutes of elliptical discussions, they finally arranged to meet face-to-face the following Thursday. He had barely cradled the phone when Darlene called through, apologising for disturbing him and wondering if he had seen *The Globe and Mail*. There was an article on new safety guidelines for pharmaceutical containers in the USA. As American pharmaceutical containers accounted for a small but significant proportion of Wentworth's market, Hart asked her to bring him the article. By the time he read it twice, it was 8:30, and the office building was filling up. Another day had begun.

Sometimes Hart thought he'd like to install a ticket machine outside his office door like those in the deli. Then simply have Darlene tell everyone to 'take a number.' This morning the first number was taken by the head of night security. 'Sorry to interrupt you, sir, but I thought I'd better report an incident last night. Some kids tried to climb the back fence at Donmar Road, the one by the loading dock.'

Wentworth didn't have enough space on the main site and rented a warehouse about five minutes away to store both materials and finished products prior to delivery. 'Did they get in?' Hart asked.

'Naw. One of the boys saw them and shone his flashlight at them. They high-tailed it off up the road. Still, thought I better tell you.'

'Have you notified the police?'

'Yep. They came and had a look around, but didn't find anything. We'll keep a good eye out tonight in case they come back. Might even be able to get hold of one of the little creeps.'

'For God's sake, don't do that,' said Hart. Night security men tended to watch too many videos. 'Just scare them off, and call the police.'

He went out to Darlene after the security man had gone and handed her the article. 'Get a copy of this over to marketing, if you would. And I'd better talk to Nick Moretti. Have you seen him yet?'

'No. Shall I page him?'

'No, he's probably in the moulding shop. I'll catch up with him when I do my tour. I'm on my way over now. If anyone calls, I'll be back in half an hour.'

'You've got letters to sign, and you have to approve the minutes of last month's board meeting,' the secretary warned.

'Half an hour. I won't forget. Hell, there's the phone. Is it for me?'

'John McTavish,' said Darlene, holding up the receiver. McTavish was an area sales manager who looked after Canada east of Ontario and New England. 'He's in Boston. He wanted Tony Leclerc, but I know for a fact Tony isn't in yet. Do you want to take it?'

'I'd better.' McTavish was in Boston chasing orders, and if he had a query it was likely to be an urgent one about production schedules and how long it would take to fill a particular order. The call took another twenty minutes, and he left for his morning tour late, knowing he would have to make up time somewhere along the way.

Wentworth Moulding's business was injection moulding. Injection moulding was at heart a relatively simple process; granular materials with the appropriate colourant added were heated until liquid and then injected into a mould where they solidified. Moulding machines varied in size, both in terms of the amount of material that could be injected in a moulding cycle and the level of locking pressure which could be applied to keep the two halves of the mould together while the material was being injected. The larger the mould, the larger the machine needed to complete the task.

Most of Wentworth's containers were of varying sizes, some of them very large. They also produced lids and tops for containers, as well as a general range of products from trays to office sundries. There were potentially thousands of products which could be produced using this process. If it could be moulded in plastic, Wentworth could make it.

Because he was short of time, Hart skipped the loading area and the mixing unit and went straight through to the moulding bays. There were 37 machines of varying sizes, and most were hard at work. Hart stopped to talk to one or two of the men on the day shift and then to Dennis Sprague, the daytime moulding manager directly responsible for keeping the machines running. 'Nick is up at the far end, if you're looking for him,' said Dennis. 'We've had a problem with # 12.'

Hart's experience told him that when two men were standing on the shop floor talking next to an idle machine, then usually the problem was serious. Nick Moretti, the manufacturing director, was standing and talking with Dave Kochner and looking at the machine standing idle. Moretti, a thin, dark man of about Hart's age, was scowling blackly. He looked up as Hart approached.

'Six hours the night shift spent on the mould change, but three out of eight impressions are defective.'

'Why didn't the night shift spot the problem in the first place?' Hart asked.

Kochner shifted. 'This was the test batch, Mr Hart. This trial run was to see if the mould was okay. We knew right away it wasn't.'

Hart looked at Moretti. 'Who supplied the mould?'

'Skillfast. That's the second dud in six months now. I'm tearing my hair out.'

'Better drop them,' said Hart.

'Hell, we can't. They're the only people in the Hamilton area who can make this kind of mould.'

'Go across the border, then. There must be someone in Buffalo.'

'Well, then you've got to pay in U.S. dollars, and that gets expensive.'

'And this isn't expensive?' Hart asked. 'What do you reckon six hours' wasted time on the night shift costs? All right. What's the name of the CEO at Skillfast? Carlson or something, isn't it? I'll ring him this afternoon.'

He left Kochner and Moretti to deal with the problem of sorting out the mess and getting the mould returned to Skillfast and went on to the assembly shop. Assembled products were another part of Wentworth's business requiring a single shift. Assembly involved putting together containers and lid assemblies and other assorted products, most of which had their origins in the mould shop. He spoke to the assembly shop manager and the quality control manager, who were checking returns, and had a look at the figures; they were good, but needed to be better.

Then he was off to the print shop. They had ten printers here and ran them on two shifts, printing moulded products according to customer requirements. The technology was silk-screen printing, but, just as the moulding shop seemed to spend a lot of its time changing moulds, so the print shop was forever switching and changing artwork. Hart checked the printing log and, as always, was surprised by the number of different orders, all with radically different run lengths. That's one of the problems with this business, he thought. Mixed order sizes gives us the worst of both worlds.

By the time he had finished in the despatch room it was nearly 11:00. The PA system crackled and Judy Salucci's voice said, 'Mr Hart, please, you're wanted at your office.'

There were two people waiting with Darlene in the outer office; Tim Pringle, who had arranged a meeting with him the previous day, and a tall man in a grey suit who produced a badge from his jacket pocket and said, 'Mr. John Hart? I'm Inspector Palliser, Ontario Provincial Police.'

Hart's first thought was that something had happened to his car, and his second thought was that something had happened to Wendy. Embarrassed at having put them in that order, he said, 'Inspector? What can we do for you?'

'I gather you've got a little security problem,' the inspector said cheerfully. Hart noticed that he had a full cup of coffee in his hand, courtesy of Darlene. He looked at Pringle, who looked back. 'All right, ' he said, a little desperately. 'Look, you'd better come into the office.'

In the office the policeman sat down, taking a gulp of his coffee. 'I thought it was important that I should come around and see you and fill you in on the situation as soon as possible. There's been a lot of vandalism in the area just now, some causing a lot of damage. We're trying to catch the kids who are doing it. We think they're the ones who tried to climb your fence last night. We'd appreciate your cooperation in sorting out this matter.'

The police were, it appeared, taking the incident at Donmar Road more seriously than Hart's own security people, and to be fair, the mess – if someone got into the warehouse and started in on the stored materials – would be expensive to clean up. Hart realised he was going to have to deal with the problem here and now. The police didn't need much, just license to come into the warehouse and have a look for themselves every few hours, but it seemed to an impatient Hart that it took forever to arrange and for the inspector to drink his coffee and be gone.

After the inspector finally left, Hart looked at Pringle and sighed, 'Couldn't he have made an appointment?'

'It's called community policing,' Pringle responded. 'Don't knock it, it might come in handy one day.'

Hart liked Pringle. Of all the senior managers, Tim was the one with whom Hart had developed the best rapport over the last six months. Nick Moretti was a difficult man to get to know; Tony Leclerc was too ambitious, and Alan Mills, the finance director, though easy-going enough, tended to keep his own counsel about anything that did not directly affect his own department. Pringle was the man who Hart found himself counting on most for an even-handed point of view. 'Tim, you wanted to see me about your training budget. What do you want to do with it?'

'Make it bigger, basically,' said Pringle. 'By about 10 percent, if possible.' He looked Hart in the eye. 'I hadn't remembered until now that we're having a board meeting later today. I should have come to see you about this earlier, but I came to discuss it as soon as I could.'

'I believe you,' said Hart, 'where thousands wouldn't. Okay, Tim, what do you want to do?'

After the personnel manager had gone, Hart reflected that Pringle, at least, had a clear idea of what he wanted to do and how he was going to do it. That was more than could be said for himself at the moment.

The board meeting, held immediately after lunch, did not do what he had hoped it would. Nick Moretti was still worrying about Skillfast and was only half there. Tony Leclerc, the marketing director, had come with a list of complaints and feedback from several customers, including Conway Foods. The annoying thing about the customer complaints was that there was no uniformity. Conway Foods was griping about delivery times, while Ekon Industries was trying to beat the price down and Dispharma had expressed concern about quality. 'I think we'll have to try and deal with these,' said Leclerc. 'We can't afford to risk losing any of these guys as customers. Conway Foods are a big customer, and I'm trying to win more orders from them. But I can't do it if I can't satisfy the demands they're already making.'

'Nick?' said Hart.

'We're running three shifts,' said Moretti. 'We're at full capacity now. Give me more moulding machines, and I could make more products and fill Conway's order faster. That's the way I see it.'

'What about the others, then?' This was Shirley Easton the development manager, Leclerc's deputy. She was one of several managers who were invited to attend board meetings on a semi-regular basis. 'Here's this other guy who is price-sensitive and doesn't need short delivery times. With Conway it's the other way around. Can't you juggle your schedule so Conway's orders get done faster?'

'I'm a production director, not a circus acrobat,' Moretti protested. 'We can play with schedules, yes, we already are, but believe me, if I could get orders done any faster I'd be doing it. I need more capacity, that's the simple answer.'

'Maybe we need more *flexible* manufacturing,' said Easton.

There was a short pause, and Hart thought about what Easton had said. 'Flexible manufacturing,' he said out loud. 'Has a good ring to it. I must remember it for the annual report.' There was laughter around the boardroom. Hart looked at Moretti. 'While we're on the subject of production standards, did you see the article in *The Globe* on new American standards for pharmaceutical containers?'

'Oh, god, yes. It had just enough information to make me aware that I need to do something, but not enough information to tell me what that something should be. Does anybody know anything about this? Shirley, have your research people heard anything?'

Easton shook her head. 'Do you suppose it's actually true?' she said doubtfully. 'I mean, how much of it do we believe?'

'Better find out,' said Hart. 'Shirley, why don't you ring *The Globe* and find out where the story comes from. The story just says it's the FDA in Washington, but there must be more to it than that.'

They got back to the agenda eventually, and moved on through maintenance reports and quality-control statistics. Tim Pringle made his case for more training money and the finance director Alan Mills, with a little prodding from Hart, agreed the money could be found.

Time dragged on and three o'clock, the scheduled end of the meeting, approached. Hart realised he hadn't even broached the subject of Wentworth's future.

At 2:50 he said,'Look, everyone, I know we're about to break up, but there's a final point I'd like to make. I want all of us to start thinking hard about something.' He looked around the table. 'I'd like to share with you a letter I received from head office this morning – not the whole letter even, just part of a statement. "Sales at Wentworth have increased but profits haven't." Everyone knows what I'm talking about.'

He scanned the table again. 'It means we have, as a company, managed to get stuck. It also means Laurentian isn't going to give us any money for capital investment, or for anything else for that matter, until the main board sees that our way forward is clear. It's up to us now to sort out this company's future.'

It was Tim Pringle who said, 'That's a bigger subject than any of us can deal with in a single meeting, John.'

'I know. That's why I am asking you all to go away and think about it. Look, I know my predecessor here, and he's a good manager. This company has not been, nor is it being, poorly run. We've got a good team, and getting this company back on track shouldn't be beyond us. I'm asking you all to start thinking about how to do it.'

There was a silence. 'Maybe we should get away from the company and meet,' said Alan Mills tentatively. 'You know, go on a management retreat or something like that.'

'Like Napoleon's retreat from Moscow,' suggested Tony Leclerc. Hart didn't laugh. 'It's an interesting idea, Alan, and one we might consider taking up later. But at the moment; well, what would we talk about? What do we talk about here? Conway Foods, defective moulds and juvenile delinquents. Won't we just go to an expensive hotel and spend a weekend talking about the same things? In my experience, that's what usually happens on management retreats. It won't get us any closer to the heart of the problem, not now.'

'I agree,' said Pringle. 'As the man who would have to organise such a junket and whose budget would have to bear the cost, I think at the moment it would not be money well spent. Look, let's all just go home and think about it. Talk it over with our spouses and our golfing partners this weekend, bat some ideas around, and let's see if anything concrete comes up. And I agree with John on another score. Five years ago this company had a sense of direction. Now, it's starting to lose it.'

15

Back in his office Hart had a quick cup of coffee and then called in Darlene to deal with the mail. There were half a dozen short letters to be written, and then he remembered Skillfast. He leaned across his desk and picked up his Rolodex and began leafing through it, looking for the Skillfast number. Finding 'S' and thumbing through, his eye fell on a card with a scribbled note in his own handwriting. It said simply, *Strategy First. Ian Macallister's firm*. There was a Montreal phone number underneath.

Hart paused for a moment. Ian Macallister was an old friend from university days; he was a Canadian who had gone to Britain to take an engineering degree, and he and Hart had moved in a lot of the same student circles. They had lost touch for a while after that, when Hart was recruited by an engineering company and Macallister went on to business school. Then, shortly after Laurentian had asked Hart to take a job in Canada, they had met again at a conference in Ottawa. They ran into each other two or three times a year now and usually had a beer for old times sake and gossiped about their jobs. Thus Hart knew that Macallister, after spells with several manufacturing companies and a few years teaching at business school, was now running his own strategy consultancy in Montreal.

Working in production, Hart had never worried much about strategy formulation, and his time in finance had not opened many more windows on the subject. Every firm had a strategy of course, and Wentworth was no exception. At the moment, however, it seemed to him that his company's strategy was to increase profits and grow. But it also seemed that this was every other company's strategy as well; in fact, it held true for almost every business. Now he was under pressure to create a strategy from scratch, at a time when his company was under both internal and external pressure to increase profits, and he was increasingly unable to articulate how he wanted to achieve his goals.

There was a lot of truth in Mike Connors' letter, he had to

admit. Wentworth was set to fall short of its profit targets for the second year running, despite continued sales growth. And he, Hart, had said nothing in his original investment proposal to allay Connors' worries on that score. After all, why *should* Laurentian give him money when they had no idea if they were going to get an acceptable return?

This was Ian Macallister's line of business. Would he perhaps have a few ideas?

He might, Hart decided after a moment, but this was his own problem and would sort it out in his own way. This was part of what being a CEO was all about; it was what he got paid for. Being new to the job he felt somewhat out of his depth. But, he would find his own way.

He found the Skillfast number and got through to the CEO. After the initial exchange of pleasantries. Hart described the faulty mould and asked how long it would be before it could be modified. Upon being told it would not be before the end of the week, he pointed out that defects were now, in his view, a serious problem and that he was giving some thought to shifting his custom elsewhere.

The CEO of Skillfast cheerfully called his bluff. 'Well, if you can afford to buy across the border in Buffalo, John, I'd say go right ahead. You get good quality over there, there's no denying it. It's just the price that everybody says is the problem.'

'Tell me which costs more,' Hart said. 'Paying a premium price, or adding up the costs of lost production. I could lose an order and even a customer over this incident, and I'm not disposed to lose more.'

The conversation ended in stalemate. Darlene rang through to say that his next appointment had arrived. By 3:30 he had the beginnings of a headache, and he still hadn't managed to do more than finish a few letters. That's the trouble, he thought. I sit here at the middle of a web, reacting to everything that comes at me. I don't initiate action, except to respond to external stimuli, phone calls, letters, appointments and people who just drop in.

He began drafting a letter to Mike Connors, thanking him for his reply and . . . what? What was he going to say or do next? The phone rang; it was Shirley Easton. 'John, I thought I'd better let you know about this FDA thing. You know, the pharmaceutical containers? Well, it's genuine. I've just been speaking to MLK, one of our customers, and they're already drawing up a note on what the changes will mean to their packaging requirements. I think we're going to need several completely new product specifications.'

'New specifications,' said Hart. 'For an existing customer, who isn't going to increase his order volume. Do they know we'll have to increase the price?'

'They won't like it,' Easton said doubtfully. 'I'd say they're pretty price sensitive already.'

After he put the phone down, Hart sat for a moment, looking out the window at the watery sunshine in the yard. The graph in his mind, with sales and profits charted on it, had altered. The two lines had just grown farther apart.

Then he pulled his Rolodex over again, picked up the phone and dialled Ian Macallister's number.

Chapter 2

"So much to do,
so little time"

At 4:45, Hart picked up the telephone again and called his wife. 'Hi! How was the opening?'

'Great,' said Wendy. She sounded exhausted. 'We sold 11 paintings and got good reviews in both *The Globe* and *The Star*. How's your day?'

'Frustrating,' said Hart, 'I've been sitting here since 7:30, and I can't actually point to one concrete achievement. It's been one damned thing after another.'

'You said on Sunday that you thought this was going to be a good week.'

'I had high expectations, but they haven't matched reality. So much to do, so little time, and not enough time to do what really needs to be done.' He paused. 'I've also done something you're not going to like. I've invited someone to stay for the weekend.'

'Who?'

Hart explained about Ian Macallister. 'He's tied up all this week and all next week. The weekend was all he could manage.'

'Well, if you expect me to stay home and be housewifely and cook you lunch, you're out of luck. I have to be in here all day Saturday, and I've a ton of paperwork for Sunday.'

'Don't worry about us. Why don't I stand us all dinner on Saturday night? You might like to meet him.'

'Why not? I could use a strategy consultant myself right about now. See you at home.'

He left the office at 5:30, having sent one final note to Pringle about Judy Salucci and her car. The weather was clouding over, and it was getting dark early. By the time he arrived home, twilight was falling over flat fields dappled with melting snow. The clouds meant warmer weather, and the snow was going quickly; already there were deep pools of standing water on the driveway.

Wendy was in the kitchen opening a bottle of white wine when he walked in and put down his coat and briefcase. He kissed her. 'You look tired.'

'I am tired. I'm off early in the morning, I'm afraid. I've got to go to London and look at the new shop and then get into

Toronto as soon as possible. I'll be late tomorrow night, too.'

He took the glass of wine she handed him, looking at her with concern. 'You're on a pretty punishing schedule.'

'Like you said, so much to do, so little time. There's much to be done, and if I don't do them, no one will. My problem is that I've overextended myself. I've got the gallery in Toronto, the restoration business, and the shops scattered between Toronto, Hamilton, Guelph, and now London.'

She raised her glass. 'Cheers. I've been thinking about this all week, I suppose in sympathy with you. I know some of the problems you tell me about sound much like some of my own, even though you can't get more different than mouldings and watercolours. But it isn't that simple, is it? It sounds like I'm simply in the art market, but originals, prints and restoration are in fact three different markets. They're three totally different businesses, come to that, which is something I certainly didn't realise when I started branching out.'

'And you're trying to ride two different horses at the same time,' Hart said.

'That's sure what it's starting to feel like. I'm not doing what I want to do any more, John. I'm doing what other people tell me to do.'

'Is there any getting away from it?' Hart asked. 'We do business in much the same way. Tony Leclerc says it's the result of being marketing-led. You know, I remember when this whole business of being marketing-led or operations-led was being thrashed out, and the marketing people swore it would lead to improved overall performance. But so far it's not worked out. Manufacturing argues it's gotten harder, not easier. Every customer wants something different. Even allowing for the bias, they have a point.'

'There's much in the maxim,' said Wendy 'about not being able to please all of the people all of the time.'

'And in trying to please all of the people all of the time, I think we're actually doing ourselves harm,' Hart said. 'Somehow we've got to find alternative ways of handling the differences that exist. There must be some other way of coping with diversity.'

'Is that what you hope this friend of yours will help you with?'

'Yes. It isn't much I need from him, just a few suggestions to get me going. I've never had to design a strategy from scratch, and I could use a few hints.'

'Well, share them around when you get them,' said Wendy. 'What's for dinner?'

Ian Macallister flew in from Montreal on Saturday morning, and Hart drove to Toronto airport to pick him up. When he drove up to 'Arrivals,' Macallister was already waiting on the sidewalk, a bag slung over his shoulder. 'Hello, Ian, hop in. How was the flight?'

'Same as it ever was,' said Macallister. 'How are you? Where's that gorgeous wife?'

'Working. How do you know she's gorgeous, you've never met her.'

'If you picked her, she's probably gorgeous,' said Macallister, 'and you're hiding her from me.'

'She picked me,' said Hart with a smile, 'and you're meeting her tonight. Right, let's go home and get some coffee.'

At the farmhouse Macallister looked around. 'Boy, this is some place. I thought when we turned off into that mudpit you call a driveway, I was going to find you living in a trailer. But this is practically a palace.'

'It was built for one of those big extended farm families, with lots of storage space for when they were snowed in all winter. That was back when Toronto was a long way off, before the 401 and QEW freeways came along and put it on the doorstep. We love it. It's got all the space we'll ever need for offices, and it's got a studio for Wendy.'

'She paints?'

'She did, when she had time.'

'What does she do now?'

Hart explained about the gallery and the chain of print shops and Macallister looked impressed. 'She built that up from scratch? That takes some doing. No wonder she doesn't have time to paint.' He took the cup of coffee Hart offered and said, 'All right, what about this company of yours? What are your problems?'

'Let's go through and sit down.'

It took some time to detail logically what he wanted to do with Wentworth and how difficult he was finding it. 'Lack of time is a big problem,' he said finally. 'But more than that, I can't seem to come to grips with the long-term running of the company. I think I'm managing it quite efficiently on a day-to-day basis, and I have firm goals. What I lack is a way to get there.'

'And how do you think I can help?' asked Macallister.

'Tell me how to go about building a strategy for Wentworth.'

On the sofa, Macallister sat and looked thoughtful. 'What are these firm goals of yours?' he asked.

'To become more profitable and to increase production capacity.'

'All right. The first thing you've got to realise is that there is no quick fix. I didn't want to say this to you on the phone because I just thought it might discourage you. But you've got to understand that I can't tell you in a weekend how to formulate a strategy. Strategy isn't an exercise you work out on a piece of paper, it's a way of thinking. It's going to take time for you to work into that.'

Hart, who had been thinking in terms of having a draft document ready by the end of the week, nodded. 'You want to increase profitability and expand production,' Macallister went on. 'Okay, let's start with the first. You want to increase profitability. What options do you have in order to do that?'

'Well . . . My first idea was that by increasing production capacity we could spread overhead and also use the opportunity to become more flexible. My development manager used a good phrase earlier in the week, "flexible manufacturing", which I think expresses what we want. You see, we receive all kinds of orders from all kinds of customers. All credit is due to marketing and sales, who work very hard, but I sometimes wish there were some way of discriminating between the kind of customer we take on. Failing that, we simply need to be able to meet our customers' demands. We need to make improvements to product quality and to the service we offer our customers. I'm quite convinced of that. My idea was to ask Group to provide capital for an expansion of facilities. Unfortunately, I've been turned down.'

'Really? Just like that?'

'No, not quite. They will fund me if I can produce a strategy that shows how I can increase profitability. I'm going in circles here.'

'Yes, you are,' said Macallister bluntly, 'and I'll tell you why. Like many companies, strategy discussions are based in generalities. You haven't said a single specific thing yet about what your strategy is aiming to achieve. Increase profitability, flexible manufacturing, improve quality – these are all just phrases. You sound like you've been reading a few textbooks.'

'In point of fact, I've read several.'

'But you haven't been able to relate the strategic concepts you've read about to your own business. You're not alone. It's an endemic problem for many firms.'

He got up and walked over to the window, looking out at the gathering grey clouds. 'It's a huge problem,' he repeated, 'and it's one I know we've got to resolve. In some ways, consultants like myself are partly to blame. We haven't explained our concepts sufficiently, and because we're trying to explain concepts to a wide audience, we have descended too far into general statements and approaches.

'It's natural, when faced with something you don't understand,' continued Macallister, 'to turn to generalities as a way forward. They seem to provide some sort of essential comfort when dealing with uncertainty. But moving on to specific strategies requires a different dimension of understanding on the part of everyone involved. And that is very complex and painstaking.

'Thus, it is typically not attempted. Too often strategy has degenerated into the task of finding all-embracing, high-sounding words and phrases that make everyone feel good. The result is that executives typically see current strategic offerings as harbingers of hope and well-being. The phrases are designed to point to answers, and the choice of words allows for generous interpretation. In fact, they can essentially mean whatever you want them to mean. Many consultants and academics now work on the premise that the more general the concept, the broader its application, and paradoxically, the more relevant it is. The path to generality has become some sort of Holy Grail; simplify everything to general concepts, hang a strategy around them and success will be yours. And, in the process, the words used have had their meanings broadened so that they can be shoe-horned into sentences and documents where they remain only marginally relevant. Definitions are now so broad that the words themselves have collapsed into meaninglessness. What does "improving customer service" really mean? Or "improving quality"? It can mean, and invariable does mean, more than one thing. People talk about improving quality in situations where quality has never really been defined. And customer service; that too is multidimensional and therefore cannot be determined without the relevant dimensions being identified.'

'That's a bit hard,' objected Hart. 'When I say I want to improve profitability, I know exactly what I mean.'

'But do your directors and managers? Does your group? Obviously not, in the latter case.'

'Surely, as you said, we're using generalisations because it helps us find common ground, to talk about and understand the same thing. Look, I'm not explaining this very well . . . We use general strategic concepts because it makes things easier, simpler.'

'But,' said Macallister, 'by resorting to generalisations you – or rather, we – are ignoring the issue of addressing difference.

We move from specific problems to generalised concepts which are supposedly relevant to any corporate situation. Thus, we are in danger of becoming simplistic. And in so doing, we make the problem still worse as essential differences are ignored. Take the Laurentian Group. If I asked whether all businesses within the Group were the same the answer would be, "no". If I then took your company and asked whether the markets served by Wentworth were the same, the answer would again be "no". If I then took one Wentworth segment and asked if all customers in that segment place the same demands on you, again the answer would be "no". So, how can a common strategy be formulated? Companies are not, therefore, whole in the sense of strategic response and approach. Core competence-type arguments are typical of today's offerings – they imply a level of commonality that does not exist. The key today, and more so in the future, is handling difference. To do that a company needs to identify difference not overlay it with generalities.'

Hart felt the ground under his feet getting softer. 'Go on,' he said.

Macallister smiled. 'Forgive me,' he said 'for displaying my deep concerns so early on. Having known you for so long, I'm speaking freely about the challenging issues of the day and setting your immediate concerns aside. However, the two are related. The order of their delivery, however, is in question.' He smiled again. 'But they are linked.

'Earlier, for example, you expressed the problems you're having in meeting customers' demands and said you thought flexible manufacturing might be a strategic response. I've heard people say similar things before, and if you'll forgive my saying this to you, it's a common response; if you don't know what your market wants, buy flexibility. Flexibility sounds good. It sounds plausible. But it does not stand up to examination. First, what do you mean by "flexibility"? It has dimensions of product range, lead time and order size. And secondly, it assumes that all markets are the same, as all apparently need the same dimensions of flexible manufacturing support.

'Many companies have, therefore, used flexibility as a strategic cop-out. What you should be thinking is, if you don't know what your markets want, find out. Companies need to move away from what is strategically superficial. They have to learn how to handle difference as well as similarity, and make the unique factors about your business and your industry work for you, not against you. And, you've got to learn to think strategically, not just think about strategy.

'That's why I say there's no quick fix,' continued Macallister. 'Look, while you were a production director or a finance director, you were a good first violinist. But now you're the composer and conductor. You've not only got to write the score, but also make sure the symphony gets played the way you and your audience want to hear it. You've got to literally be in tune with your markets. That's a sizeable leap in terms of task and thinking.'

'I suppose it is. And yes, I'll confess I was looking for a quick solution. I was hoping an expert would come along and tell me what I have to do.'

'I can only tell you what I believe you have to do,' said Macallister. 'And one of those things is to rely on your own point of view, not that of an outside expert. You have to develop a strategy which is completely interwoven with your own job and your own company. When it comes to the crunch, John, your main personal role is to provide and manage strategy. You have directors to look after the functional side of the business; they look to you to provide overall direction. But you can't lead them anywhere until you know where you want to go.'

Macallister looked out the window again. 'Is there somewhere we can go for a walk? I feel better talking about these things in the fresh air.'

Outside there was a wet wind blowing in their faces. They walked across the muddy field beside the house, climbing a low hill. 'Looks like spring is finally on its way,' observed Hart. 'I like a lot of things about this country, but I still find the winters hard to get used to. Every year when the snow melts, I feel like the whole world is changing.'

'That's the good thing about it,' said Macallister. 'I wouldn't want to live in the tropics where the weather was always the same. I like the ebb and flow of the seasons, it helps mark the passage of time.'

'The passage of time is something I prefer not to be reminded of,' said Hart. 'If someone offered me the chance to go and manage a plant in Bermuda, I think I'd take it.'

Macallister laughed. 'That's a revealing statement! You'd like to live in Bermuda, but you'd still want to be in manufacturing. What would you make, beach huts?'

'Why not? There's probably a market. I trained as an engineer, remember. I'm not happy unless I'm making something.'

'Well, good for you,' said Macallister. 'That's the right attitude to start with.'

'Is it? I'm not so sure. We ran our manufacturing industries for decades on the basis that we liked to make things, so we dreamed up all sorts of products and then went out and tried to sell them to markets that didn't exist. I hope we've learned from our marketing people that the end object is to sell things, not make things, but most of us are happier with processes than with marketing. I look at people like Tony Leclerc, my marketing director, and think that he probably has more influence on how the company is run than I do.'

Macallister stopped. 'Are you serious?'

'Semi. We're marketing-led, it's our proud boast, and it's true. We respond to the needs of the market. We react as the market requires us to react.'

'Do you? Or do you react as your marketing department requires you to react?'

'What's the difference?'

'Between being "marketing-led" and "market-led"? Quite a lot. Are you driven by the needs of the market, or by the need of your marketing department to increase sales? Because that's what marketing departments typically see as their goal; not to increase profits, but to increase sales. And that's how it works. They bring in orders, and it's up to the rest of the company to ensure that those orders are filled profitably.'

'As I remember,' said Hart, 'the AMA's definition of marketing is "meeting customer needs, *profitably*." Surely the notion of profit is inherent in a marketing function's work.'

'But, how does your marketing department define the word "profitably"? We're back to generalisations again. Is it "any order with the potential to make a profit", or "orders which *maximise* profit"?'

Hart didn't answer. Macallister went on, 'If you extend the marketing argument far enough, you reach the classic statement that the customer is always right. But this is manifestly untrue. What many companies have lost sight of is that it is they who are responsible for their own strategies, and it is they who determine which customers to supply and which set of needs to meet. This does not mean that the customer is a passive player, far from it. But the initial decisions on which customers to supply is made by the company. Once that decision is made, then, yes, the company has to supply the needs of the customer. But by this point what the customer's needs are has been accepted and agreed to and is monitored by both parties.

'This in fact moves the relationship between company and customer away from the classic buyer-seller relationship to something more like a supplier-partner arrangement. But we're getting away from the subject at hand. The question I usually ask companies at this stage is, how well do you know your markets? I don't mean how well does your marketing director know them, but how well do you yourself know them?'

'Well, I've only been there four months. I know roughly what segments we sell into. Food and beverage containers are two of the biggest, along with cosmetics and general industrial containers. Those can be for anything, but our biggest customers are chemical companies. How many have I mentioned, four?

The fifth is household products: that's also quite big, and then there's a catch-all segment for sundry products. Six in all.'

'And that's how you define your markets? By the end user or the product description?'

'At the moment, yes.'

Macallister was standing on top of the little hill, hands in his jacket pocket and looking out to the south toward the lake. 'It's this whole problem of markets,' he said, and for a moment Hart thought he was talking to himself. 'For a long, long time, markets were stable. They grew, but they were stable in nature, and you could count on finding yourself a spot where, so long as you produced good quality at a competitive price, you could, in theory, carry on forever.

'That was in the days, when demand exceeded supply, and simple growth was the most effective strategy there was. Some time in the last couple of decades that all began to change. For a variety of reasons, markets started to become less stable. Now, markets are dynamic, markets change faster than products, products change faster than processes, and processes change faster than buildings and layout. We're now working in a state of flux.

'I think it was because market conditions were changing while manufacturing was remaining the same, or at least failing to catch up, that people started thinking that perhaps manufacturing had had its day, and that the future lay with services. At first services seemed like the path of least resistance. Not much was known about them, and there was plenty of room for the theoreticians to postulate about service strategies. Services were growing, and just as in manufacturing's golden age, demand was outstripping supply.

'What has been brought back into focus is simply that, by and large, manufacturing is wealth-creating whereas services recycle wealth.

'So,' Macallister concluded, 'we've got to do something to sort out manufacturing's problems and get it back on the right track. We've got to explore new ways of looking at the world from manufacturing's point of view.'

'You want me to redefine my markets,' said Hart.

Macallister laughed. 'Yes,' he said, 'Yes, I do, among other things. That's a good place to start.'

'I can see that,' Hart said slowly. 'If I'm to change the way I think about my business, I shall have to change the way I think about my markets. What else?'

'You'll have to change the way you think about your company as well. You'll have to get used to the mantle of the strategic role. Setting goals is easy. Achieving goals is difficult. Setting them *and* achieving them is the most difficult thing of all.'

'Now look who's talking in platitudes,' Hart said dryly. Macallister laughed again. 'Touché. But what I'm driving at is this. We've realised that we need to revitalise our manufacturing industries, but we haven't come up with the strategies to do so; we've talked a lot about things like "world class manufacturing", but these are more cliches. They're used as surrogates for real strategy.

'Strategy encompasses a company and its markets and welds them together. Strategic thinking is proactive, not reactive, and seeks to put a company into markets where it is both profitable and effective with a clear eye on the future. To do all this means hard work. The level of understanding, the clear recognition of differences and marshalling functional strategies to support these directions is a tough task to bring about.

'The first stage is to become market-driven. Then, you've got to drive the market. How much longer can you afford to wait and let the vagaries of changing markets toss Wentworth around until its production facilities can no longer cope with demands? Or can you take command, increase the company's control over what it wants to do, and put it into the markets where you want it? If that sounds like a challenge, then it is. You've been a bean counter for long enough, John. It's time you chose the game, agreed the rules and kept score.'

Chapter 3

"Strategy is a way of thinking"

They spent the rest of the afternoon in the house, in Hart's study. He gave Macallister some of the documents he himself had been given when he took over, including annual reports and valuations, and they spent several hours discussing Wentworth and its business.

'So,' said Macallister, 'you've got three basic processes, moulding, printing and assembly. Within those you've got a variety of different product specifications, each requiring its own alteration to the process. Different moulds, different printing designs and so on.'

'That's right. The technical details don't really matter, so I'll just explain that on the moulding side we use everything from single cavity moulds that make just one large container up to 64-cavity moulds that might be used to make lids or bottle tops. Only the big machines can run the big moulds, and they take longer to change over, eight hours, typically, whereas a small machine takes less than an hour.'

"We never produce any one product continuously. We don't have the demand. However, the frequency of repeat orders and the order quantities involved vary significantly. Our work comprises custom products in that they need to meet the specific requirements of customers, but in no way are they specials. To the production process, be it moulding, printing or assembly, all products are standard products. We merely set up the process according to the moulding or printing or assembly requirements specified by the customer. And, rarely is a product only ordered once.'

He paused. 'Like most businesses, ours uses a batch process. The volume is insufficient to use line, so we use batch. Over the years we have worked very hard at improving efficiencies and reducing set-ups.'

'And these three processes, moulding, printing and assembly. They're organised into separate units?'

'Well, yes. That's standard procedure, it allows for economies of scale and for concentration of expertise in particular fields.'

'And all your support services and other functions, these are organised as separate departments as well?'

'Yes, of course. Why are you asking me all this?'

'How good would you say communications are between departments?' Macallister asked, ignoring the question.

'Not as good as they should be, but then they never are. We could do a lot more to ensure that different areas know what the others are doing, but time is a factor. All the people I have working for me are specialists, in one way or another. It's difficult for them to keep up with other aspects of the business when they have their heads down concentrating on their own jobs.'

Macallister nodded. 'Sure. Different departments, all separate and hierarchical. Design and development, manufacturing, accounting/finance, human resources and marketing – all in a little box somewhere on the left side of the diagram.' He turned over a memo on production figures and began drawing on the back of it. 'It all looks like this, a horizontal row of boxes, representing functional strategies, with a corporate strategy statement that's supposed to link them together.'

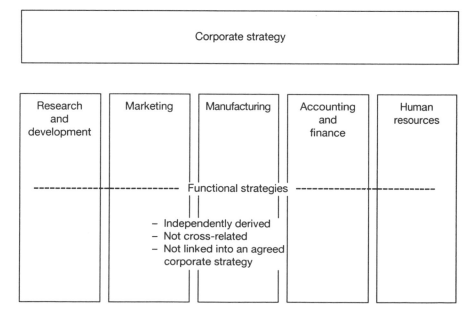

'And you're going to tell me that's wrong,' said Hart.

'I'm going to ask you to think about whether it's right,' said Macallister. 'Like I said this morning, strategy is a way of thinking. You have to develop the frame of mind, John, where you can examine *everything* about your company down to the last nut and bolt and see whether its design reflects your goals for the company. Then, you change the things that require change, and you can keep changing them and developing them into the future. If that means solutions that may seem unconventional or radical to someone on the outside, well, so be it. It's only right if it's right for you.'

Hart nodded slowly. 'Okay. It's taken you most of the day, but you've convinced me that I'm going to have to start thinking strategically.'

'Don't belittle the step you've made. Some managers go through their entire working lives and never understand that. You'll be all right, but it's going to take some time. Again, there are no quick fixes. This is going to be a process of several months, or more, depending on you and your top managers. Are you willing to bring me in?'

'I'll have to let Group know,' Hart said, 'but I don't expect they'll raise any objections. Are you willing to take me on?'

The two men shook hands, solemnly. 'Right,' said Hart. 'Where do I have to start?'

'Where everybody has to start. With your markets. I'll repeat a question I asked this morning. How well do you understand your markets?'

'By the criteria you've set,' Hart said slowly, 'not well enough. If I'm to start thinking about whether everything in my company is geared to doing what I want it to do, and if all my goals for the company are based on the market; then, no, I can't see my way ahead. I've got some learning to do.'

'Well done!' Hart looked up in surprise; Macallister was laughing at him. 'You just climbed the first hurdle. Okay, it's time to come to grips with your markets. I want you to set up a meeting with me and your top people as soon as you can, preferably within the next two weeks. I want to hear them tell me in their own words how Wentworth sees its markets and what its marketing strategy is, and I want us to have a chance to discuss that strategy in detail. Can that be arranged?'

'It can. I'll contact you as soon as we have some possible dates; I'll need to give my marketing people some time to prepare. If we explain how we segment our markets and describe each segment, along with figures like market growth and gross contributions, would that be sufficient?'

'It would be a start, yes. Then the next stage is to proceed with some more in-depth analysis. I'll explain what you need to do when we meet.'

'The next stage,' said Hart, 'is to get into Toronto, pick up my wife, and have dinner. I'm sorry to cut you off, Ian, but I'm also beginning to see what you mean about this being a long process. You've given me more than enough to think about, and I want to mull it over for a while.'

Driving into Toronto in the early evening, Macallister talked about his own company and how it was expanding, slowly but steadily. 'I made a conscious decision to focus on manufacturing companies,' he said. 'I'm also running counter to the perceived wisdom about how a consultant should operate. A lot of people call me in expecting quick fixes, and I uniformly disappoint them.'

'That's not very market-driven of you, Ian. Don't they just find someone who will tell them what they want to hear?'

'Some of them do,' said Macallister. 'And some of them phone me back a year later and say, "Ian, I hate to admit it, but you were right." You see, I don't tell people how to do things; I tell them how to figure out how to do things for themselves. That's a lot harder, both for me and the other people involved. But, it's a good job to be doing. I love manufacturing, but when I ran plants, I always came across the same problem – independent functional strategies lacking discussion, agreement and subsequent coherence. And business school was a worthwhile experience, but I found the same problems there; everything is divided up by functions. Business is taught by separate subject areas, and specialists rule.

'But the combination of the two experiences helped me see clearly; first, what I thought manufacturing companies shouldn't be doing and then, a long time later, what maybe they should be doing. There is one thing I've learned that the outside consultant or expert can do that is more valuable than anything else, and that is offer a dispassionate long-term opinion. So many people find that hard to take from the inside.'

'My God, yes,' Hart said. 'You're in the thick of it all the time. There just isn't the time to sit down and plan. It's a constant struggle, the scramble to get orders and then to fill them, to find more and bigger customers and then keep them happy. And it doesn't get easier to find time as you go up the ladder, it gets harder.'

'That's a classic problem,' said Macallister. 'You were a good specialist manager, John; you must have been, or they wouldn't have given you a company the size of Wentworth. I think Laurentian picked you because they thought you could keep your head above water.'

'They as much as told me so on my first day,' Hart pulled out to change lanes, passing a tanker. The CN tower was clearly visible ahead, and the skyscrapers of downtown Toronto were coming into view. 'I thought it was an exciting prospect, to be honest. This was the job I had wanted for the last 15 years. Now, it's just worrying. I wanted this job, Ian, and I still want it, and I'm proud of the fact that I've got my own company, and I want to be a success. But I'm torn in two.'

'Because of your wife?'

'It's more complicated than that. She works as hard as I do, if not harder; it's difficult for us to have a life together. We're both doing what we're doing because we want to succeed. Money matters, I'll not deny that, but. . . . We want to get somewhere in life.'

'But not at any cost.'

'No, there are limits to the sacrifices we can make. We both drove ourselves when we were younger. She didn't marry at all, never had the chance to have a relationship or have kids, and I married and it fell apart six years later. I used to work every evening at home until midnight, and every Saturday and most Sundays. I suppose if I wanted to I could do that again now, and maybe then I could secure the time I needed to take this dispassionate long-term view. But I doubt it. More time would probably just add up to more phone calls and more paper work.'

'Almost certainly,' agreed Macallister. 'And you don't have to work around the clock in order to develop a strategic point of view. By the time I've finished with you, you'll be living and breathing strategy all the time, and you won't need to do that on top of everything else. It won't be the job plus strategy. The job itself will *be* strategy.'

'Do you give money-back guarantees on that?' asked Hart. Macallister only laughed. 'There is one other thing. I'm certain of you, but what about your senior managers? Are you happy with them?'

'Oh, yes. Very.'

'Will they back you? And will they understand what you want to do?'

'Yes. Nick Moretti, the manufacturing director, is a chronic pessimist, but he's bright. He's quick to see opportunities, even if he's equally quick to think of reasons why they will fail.'

'I remember you when you were a manufacturing director,' said Macallister. 'Pessimism seems endemic in manufacturing directors. It must come from having to do six impossible things before breakfast, day in and day out. It's also one of the reasons why so many manufacturing companies don't fulfill their potential. Production is at the heart of any manufacturing company, yet most manufacturing directors spend all their time responding to the other parts of the business. They're constantly reactive, because they don't have time to be anything else. Unfortunately that attitude has now become institutionalised, and both production managers and other parts of the company expect this reactive stance.'

'That's about the size of it,' agreed Hart. 'On the other side, my marketing director is very proactive, and very good. Tony Leclerc is a ball of fire. Talk about energy, I wish I had half his. Unfortunately, I'm about to lose him, but I've been lucky enough to find a very able replacement on hand, if she'll take the job.'

'You'd better start bringing her into things as soon as possible, then,' said Macallister. 'It's not just you that has to become strategically oriented, John, it's the whole company. Strategy starts with you, and flows through your top managers. She'll have to be in the process of development. And this marketing and manufacturing thing will have to be addressed soon. It's no good treating these two functions like an old married couple, with marketing going out to work every day and manufacturing staying home doing the housekeeping. They both have basic roles to play in supporting the business. Agreeing on the market and on their respective roles to support these agreed-upon needs is one of the keys to a successful business.'

They parked the car at Eaton's Centre and walked to the gallery. Chope Gallery's central location was the lower floor of an office building, a broad open room hung with paintings and interspersed with sculpture groups. An enormous tapestry hung from the ceiling; behind it was a mezzanine where smaller works were displayed and where Wendy had her suite of offices. She was on the telephone when Hart and Macallister came up the stairs, but waved them in.

'Yes, I'll call you on Monday, Alec. We didn't sell any of your work, I'm afraid, but there are several people interested. You might be able to get a commission out of this, at least. Yes, all right, good luck. Bye.'

She hung up, and clasped her hands firmly in front of her on the desk. She was trying to give up smoking. 'This must be the famous Mr. Macallister.'

Hart introduced them. 'All right,' said Wendy, 'I'm about through. I think we should all go along to the Royal York and have a drink.'

The bar of the Royal York was filled with weekend refugee shoppers rather than its usual weekday population of dealers from Bay Street. They ordered drinks. Wendy said, 'Ian, I hope you don't mind, but I've invited a date for you tonight.'

'My girlfriend lives and works in New York,' Macallister said, 'so I should be safe enough.'

'Who did you ask?' asked Hart.

'Donna Kovalek.' She turned to Macallister. 'She's a good friend of mine, runs a very successful travel agency in a location not too far from me. Actually I owe her a dinner anyway, and I thought this was a good chance to slip it in on John's bill. What did you think of my gallery, Ian?'

'I'm not very well educated about art,' he said thoughtfully, and picked up his martini. 'But the setup is very impressive. That's a great room.'

'It should be. It costs me an arm and a leg in rent. But it's my central showcase, and I've got to keep it.'

'Where else do you have galleries?'

'That's the only real art gallery I have. I have a picture restoration business, which I also run out of that site, using restorers working on contract. Then I have five small shops which are a combination of print galleries and picture framing shops, mostly in shopping malls. I've got outlets in North York, Oakville, Mississauga, Hamilton and Guelph, and I'm about to open a sixth in London.' She raised her glass. 'We crossed the million dollar mark last year.'

'That's very good going,' said Macallister.

'Yeah, well. Blood and toil, sweat and tears, as the man said, and you can get pretty well anywhere.'

'The blood and the tears are mostly other people's,' said Hart, and Wendy laughed. 'Yes, being aggressive and manipulative helps too, especially when you work with artists.'

41

'I thought artists were all terribly cerebral types, interested in their art alone. You know, competely unworldly and unable to deal with money.'

'It's a touching point of view,' Wendy conceded, 'and one I am occasionally able to turn to my advantage. People are less likely to complain about the price of a sculpture if they think the sculptor is innocent and unworldly. It works in our favour from time to time. Ah, here comes Donna.'

Hart knew Donna Kovalek well; she was a relaxed, cheerful woman who neither looked nor acted like a successful, high-powered travel agent. 'Sit down and have a drink, Donna,' he said after the introductions were over. 'We were just talking about deceiving our customers. Any thoughts on the subject?'

Donna made a face. 'I would never knowingly deceive a customer of mine,' she said virtuously, 'despite the fact that the airlines practise deceit on me on a regular basis. No, seriously, there's no point. In a service business, people have to know exactly what they're getting. Quality is built almost entirely on expectations, and I've got to match those expectations as far as possible.'

'But what if your different customers have different expectations?' asked Macallister. 'I assume that business travellers and leisure travellers exhibit quite different types of behaviour and have quite different expectations. It isn't just as simple as getting bums on seats, is it?'

'No,' Donna agreed. 'So, you have to segment your bums a little more carefully. We offer two different services in my business, two different packages, two different marketing programmes, two different kinds of ads, two different bundles of benefits, not to mention two different prices. It all starts with the same basic product, just a seat on an airplane that's going some place, but by tinkering with the details, we can make it more or less attractive to one group or the other and then sell it directly to them.

'Sure,' said Wendy. 'I do the same. I sell originals by respected artists in the big gallery to people who are serious collectors, or at least art fanciers and sometimes to corporations looking for an investment and a status symbol. Then I sell frames and prints in the suburbs to middle-income customers who want something nice to hang on their wall. Sometimes they're even the same work of art; an original oil might go for $5000 in the gallery, and prints of the same painting might sell for $75 or $150 in Oakville. Same arrangement of colours, different market.'

'Same arrangement of colours?' said Donna skeptically. 'That's a little cynical, Wendy. What happened to the cerebral factor, the unconscious desire to possess, the spark of intuition through which a customer is attracted to a work of art and decides to buy it – be it a $5000 mural or a $10 print? That's a direct quote from your annual report, by the way.'

'I know it is,' said Wendy. 'I mean it's the same basic product, like you sell seats on airplanes and John makes plastic containers and Ian – what's your basic product, Ian?'

'Hot air, some would say,' said Macallister. 'Go on. You were saying?'

'In my business, a product only has value if it has meaning for people. That's why Donna objects to me calling paintings an arrangement of colours. "Colour" itself is a pretty loaded word. You wouldn't catch two artists talking about something being "red" in a painting, they would each have totally different ideas about what "red" is. They might say that there were a lot of "reds" in that painting, but they would be talking about a generalised impression that would have nothing to do with technique or appeal. Now the general public isn't that sophisticated, and every month I have someone come in and ask for a nice green painting that will match the hall carpet, but even that's only a starting point. They eventually take a painting away because it appeals to them, not because it's green.'

She finished her drink. 'At least, most of them do.'

'I do believe the three of you cooked this up beforehand,' Hart said. 'Ian and I were just talking this afternoon about markets and how you define them, and I confessed that I was

43

going to have to go away and take another look at mine because I didn't really understand them. Here you and Donna sit with it all at your fingertips. I should have called you in as consultants and left Ian in Montreal.'

'But then we wouldn't be going out for dinner,' said Donna, 'and we'd be at home with nothing to do this evening. So actually you've done us a great service by bringing Ian down. Personally, I am not going to talk about business any more at all this evening. Can someone ask the waiter if he knows the score in the hockey game?'

They didn't talk business any more, which to Hart was a relief. They talked about England, Montreal, and the forthcoming provincial elections, and had an enjoyable evening. Hart, who drank little in any case, stuck to mineral water while the other three split a bottle of wine, and he drove with Wendy and Macallister back to the house, arriving late.

It was not until they had seen Macallister off to bed and were getting into their own bed upstairs that Wendy said quietly, 'How is it going?'

'Okay, I think. He is really a big help. He's showing me that I have to think differently about the business, and he is helping me overcome this fear of not having enough time. That's the biggest thing of all. I was getting quite wound up about the fact that there was never enough time to do everything.'

'I know. You were like a kid with a new toy when you got this company, for the first week or so. Then it was a little like you'd discovered the toy didn't work properly. You've looked troubled ever since.'

'I was worried. I still am. I have to say that letter from Mike Connors earlier in the week, telling me I couldn't have the investment money, really took the wind out of my sails. I had been proceeding on the assumption that most of our problems could be solved if we could only produce more, and we could get bigger customers and fill bigger orders. The fact that I was being turned down, even only conditionally, made everything seem twice as hard.'

'So will Ian help you manage without the investment?'

'I don't want him to do that. I still want that money, Wendy, and I want Wentworth to grow, a long way. But I need a plan, a strategy, both in order to unlock Laurentian's coffers and get the money out, and to grow the company. I can see that now, and I can understand why Mike Connors said no; because they couldn't see what they were going to get back on the deal.'

'And now you think you can persuade them?'

'I damned well will persuade them. All my ambitions are still there, Wen. This is my first company, and I'm going to take it places.'

Chapter 4

"Markets are inherently dynamic, while manufacturing is inherently fixed"

David Clarkson, the managing director of Conway Foods, was much more genial in person that he had seemed on the phone. A thickset, balding man in his early fifties, wearing a check sports jacket, he breezed into Hart's office on Thursday afternoon and held out a broad hand. 'Hi, John. Good to meet you. I always figure it's better to get these problems thrashed out face to face.'

Hart, who had been prepared to dislike Clarkson on sight, instead found himself warming to this good-natured man who was, after all, facing many of the same problems that he himself faced. He introduced his team; Tony Leclerc was there as a matter of course, but Hart had also called in Nick Moretti on a stroke of inspiration as well. Darlene brought in a tray of coffee, and Clarkson drank his appreciatively.

'Well, boys. Here's the picture the way I see it. We've been doing business for about four years now, and so far I'd say Conway Foods has been satisfied with what we've got. I'm not saying we couldn't do better with a different supplier, but at the same time I'm not totally confident that we could go out and find a better supplier tomorrow. So far, I haven't believed that it was worth the effort for me to do so. So there's no reason, from my point of view, why we can't go on having a satisfactory business relationship.'

The other three nodded, waiting. 'But,' Clarkson went on, 'there's one thing you fellows have got to understand, and that's the kind of pressure I'm facing in my business. I'm in a market that's moving and shifting all the time, never the same from one day to the next. So I have to be developing new products, *and* repacking existing products to meet customer demand – that's demand from the retailers, who think they understand the nature of demand from the ultimate customers – *and* trying to cope with new regulations on hygiene and what have you that affect the standards of what I produce. And that affects you guys who supply my packaging just as much as it affects the actual food suppliers.'

'I think we do understand that,' Hart said. 'We try to remain as flexible as possible to meet demands from our customers, people like yourselves. But we can't always respond instantly to any new demand.'

'Well, I need instant, or pretty close to instant, support a lot of the time,' Clarkson said. He took another drink of his coffee. 'Look, I'll lay my cards on the table. My company is thinking of making a big move into a new range of foods. While we're in the process of entering the market, we're going to be trying a lot of different ranges, and that means different container sizes and shapes, most of them printed, we don't know yet, and maybe short runs in a hurry. Now I realize that means we will be upsetting your schedules, and we're prepared to pay a reasonable price to get the containers – so long as they arrive on time and according to government health standards. Can you guarantee we'll be satisfied?'

This, Hart knew, was the big new order Leclerc had been trying to win from Conway. He looked at Nick Moretti. The manufacturing director was in turn looking at Leclerc. 'Well,' he said. 'I'd have to see the specifications of course, especially on volume, which I assume Tony will get from your buyers. But, yes, with enough advance notice, we can meet your orders. Our biggest delay will be in getting moulds made, and then testing those moulds in production. Once we've tested we can produce as fast as you want.'

Clarkson finished his coffee. 'That doesn't sound real definite, Nick. What kind of notice are we talking about here?'

'The biggest time factor is getting moulds,' Hart cut in. 'We use three or four different suppliers for those, and all seem to take about the same length of time.' He neglected to mention that they were also having reliability problems with one supplier. 'We are working on cutting down that time, but the only option at the moment seems to be to go over the border to Buffalo, and that means an extra cost which, I'm afraid, we have to pass onto the customer.'

'Tell you straight,' said Clarkson. 'I'm not going to pay an unreasonable price, because I've got my own margins to look after. But at the same time, having a hundred thousand chicken Kiev and green beans stuck in my process because I don't have the packaging to put them in isn't too good for my margins either. I can afford to pay for promptness. I don't want to be unreasonable about this, so anything I can do to help you fellows, let me know.'

"There is one thing,' Hart said suddenly. 'Nick wants some samples of product specs and volumes, but I'd like your own estimate of what the likely ongoing volume of orders for these new containers will be, and some idea of the ceiling you think you can afford to pay. It's a very attractive-looking piece of business, I agree, but I think we need to look at it from a few different angles before we commit ourselves to taking it.'

He sensed Leclerc become suddenly tense beside him, and even Moretti gave him a sideways look. Clarkson, however, looked as genial as ever. 'Seems reasonable. I'll get some facts and figures faxed over to you tomorrow morning. Everything's provisional of course, you realise that.'

'Of course," said Hart. 'Even so, that will be a big help.'

After Clarkson had been shown out, Hart walked over to the window of his office and stood looking at the afternoon sun glancing off the windows across the yard. Leclerc came in behind him and said, 'Got a minute, John?'

'Tony, come in, Want another coffee?'

Leclerc shook his head. 'I'll only be a minute. I just wondered if you were happy with this Conway order.'

'In theory I am. But I want to take a closer look. I'm worried about Nick, and whether he can take on this kind of job. If it's all low-volume, short lead-time orders, it will play hell with his production schedules. And that could mean we keep Conway while losing other customers. Can we afford to do that?'

'Conway is an important customer,' Leclerc said slowly. 'And so far, they've been a good one. We've gotten a lot of business from them.'

'I know we have; I've looked at the figures. I just hope we can give them what we want. I'm not at all sure we can.'

Leclerc nodded slowly. Hart said, 'This may seem sudden, but I think it's about time we started asking realistic questions about what we can and cannot do. Look at Nick, sitting there nodding his head and doing whatever the customer wants: I did it myself when I was in the same job. You're dying to say no; we're overstretched already and we can't possibly begin to take on any more customers, but you can't say no. You know that you need new business; you've got to have it, it's like oxygen to your company. Well, too much oxygen can be just as fatal as too little.'

'It sure can,' said Leclerc. 'So what do you want to do? Start reviewing our marketing strategy and see if we can see from that where we're going wrong?'

'Yes,' said Hart, 'that's exactly what I want to do. As I said on Monday, I'm bringing in a consultant to help us out with strategy. Before he comes, I want a full review of our marketing strategy. Then I want the three of us to meet before the consultant comes.'

'How soon do you want to do this?'

'Very soon. I'm trying to get the consultant down to meet with all of us on Thursday. I want Shirley to be there.'

'I've got to go to Montreal, and I won't be back until Tuesday, so I won't have a lot of time. I might have to put Shirley onto this full-time.'

'Do that. It's time she started learning along with the rest of us.' He looked up at Leclerc. 'Have you heard anything yet about your new job?'

Leclerc grinned. 'It's like being in the navy again, and waiting for your next posting. You'll probably hear before I do, John.'

'Well, keep me posted,' said Hart. 'I'd rather not lose you just at this precise moment, but if I am going to, I want Shirley ready to step straight into your shoes.'

Friday passed uneventfully except for a telephone call to Mike Connors at Laurentian. Connors' Virginia twang came onto the line almost straight away. 'How are you, John? Freezing to death up there?'

'No, the thaw seems set to last. I've got green patches in the fields around the house.'

'That's good. What can I do for you?'

'Mike, I've received your letter, and you've probably received my reply. But I need to make you a proposition. If I can show you a strategic plan that proves I can improve Wentworth's profitability, can I have the investment I asked for?'

'Sure,' said Connors laconically. 'If the plan looks good, then yeah, we'll give you the money. When can we expect to see something on paper.'

'Three months,' said Hart, suddenly aware of feeling happier than he had in a long time.

'Great,' said Connors. 'Best of luck.' And that was that.

He arrived home just behind Wendy and drove up the muddy driveway behind her and followed her into the carport. 'There's timing for you,' he said. 'Come on, let's go in and have a drink before we start thinking about dinner.'

They went into the house and began turning on lights. 'We need a housekeeper,' Wendy said. 'Think how nice it would be to come home at night and have dinner already cooking.'

'No housekeeper would face that driveway,' Hart said, making for the bar. 'They'd all quit. Glass of wine, or whisky?'

'Scotch for me. You're in a good mood today.'

'I am,' he said, and told her about his call to Connors. She sat down on the sofa, putting her feet up and watching him as he talked, and at the end she said, 'So. You've got it, then?'

'Yes, or I will have in three months.'

'Ian Macallister's done you a lot of good,' she said. 'A week ago, you didn't think you could ever do what had to be done for Wentworth. Now you're confident you can. That's a big difference in a short space of time.'

'There's more than that,' he said. 'I realised, driving home, that I'm making progress in the company. I'm meeting Tony

Leclerc and Shirley Easton on Monday to do a complete review of all our markets. That's something I should have done weeks ago, but I didn't do it because I didn't have time.'

'And now you do?'

'No. I'm busier than ever. But this now seems like one of the most important things I can do, a key part of my job, not part of some extra activity to be squeezed in when I have the time. I'm realising what Ian meant when he said strategy had to become part of my job.'

'Can I ask a question?' she asked. 'You're asking your marketing people to review your markets, but why not your production people too? After all, it's on them that meeting the market's demands depend, isn't it?'

He stared at her. 'If I had a customer who wanted a picture restored,' she said, 'I wouldn't say yes until my restorer had a look at it and pronounced it possible. Okay, maybe it's not a very apt analogy. But from the outside, it seems to me to make sense.'

'Yes,' he said. 'It does. You wouldn't like to come and work for an injection-moulding company, would you?'

'No,' she said firmly. 'I feel like a steak to-night. How about you?'

They enjoyed a quiet weekend and Wendy even spent most of Sunday afternoon in her studio, working on an oil landscape she'd had in progress for months. Hart enjoyed watching her paint; she seemed to work with only half her mind on palette and easel, yet every brushstroke was sure and precise. The magic of painting, the layering of pure color that gradually took on solid form, was something he could appreciate without fully understanding it.

'How's your London store going?' he asked.

'Grand opening is next Saturday. Can you come?'

'Free champagne? I wouldn't miss it. So where next for Chope Galleries? Waterloo, Windsor, Sarnia? Ottawa?'

'Ottawa,' she said. 'But I want to do something different in Ottawa. I'm not sure what yet.'

'You've got a good thing going with the print and frame shops. Why not replicate it?'

'Ottawa's different. It's the capital, and there's a lot more money and a variety of different tastes there. There are more tourists, too. It's a different kind of market. We might put a print and frame shop in a suburban mall, but I want to get a downtown site, as close to Parliament Hill as possible.'

Hart drove to work on Monday morning feeling more relaxed than he had in some time. In the middle of the morning, he picked up the phone and dialled Ian Macallister's number. Macallister himself answered the phone. 'Being your own office boy these days?' asked Hart.

'Practically. My secretary is in bed with flu, and I was just on my way out, so you're lucky to get anyone at all. Are we still on for Thursday?'

'Thursday at 2:00. I've told everyone this is going to be only a review session, where we present our current marketing strategy and ask you for comment. Is that what you want?'

'That's okay for now. I will almost certainly ask your marketing people to go away and come back with more information, so at the end of Thursday's meeting we'll want to fix a time for a second meeting.'

'Fine. See you Thursday.'

'Give my regards to your charming wife,' said Macallister, and rang off.

He arrived just after lunch on Thursday. Hart saw him from his office window and, watching him pay his cab driver, pick up his briefcase and walk towards the office building. He felt his stomach tighten. He wondered if perhaps it would have been better to have used a stranger. Putting yourself on show like this before a friend brought added difficulty.

When he came in Macallister was relaxed and easy. Darlene Myers, having been introduced, asked him how he took his coffee. He dropped his briefcase by the door and went over to stand by the window. 'So, this is where it all happens, eh?'

'Not a bit of it,' said Hart. 'I'll show you where it all happens, if you like, after you've had your coffee. Do you want a tour?'

'I'd like one, yes. Do you want me to meet anyone before the meeting?'

'Not unless you want to.' Hart hesitated. 'I have to tell you that this may not be as smooth a meeting as I thought when I first called you. I thought we'd have some firm conclusions for your comments. But quite a lot has changed in the last week. Now I'm starting to think I may have called you too soon. I hope I'm not wasting your time.'

'No, I shouldn't think you are. Early involvement is necessary as a way of getting across concepts and new approaches, and it's also high time I met your team and formed my own conclusions. Is everyone suddenly being stricken with doubt?'

'Some of us are.' Hart said, a little grimly, 'and some of us ought to be, but aren't. I asked everyone to go away and think of what the important elements in our strategy ought to be. Apart from everyone coming up with different conclusions, my manufacturing director seems to have got it into his head that strategy is something that the marketing department and I have to sort out and that his only role is to respond to what we tell him to do.'

'And you're surprised at this?' asked Macallister. 'Three or four years ago when you ran manufacturing, if you'd been in this situation, what would you have done?'

'The same, I suppose,' Hart said tiredly. 'No, that's not true. I would have tried, I think – I hope – to seek ways in which my department could contribute to the strategic process. I would have tried to ensure that manufacturing played its own strategic role.'

'Mmm,' said Macallister. 'That could be why you're now a CEO and not still a manufacturing director.'

The door opened and Darlene came in with two cups of coffee. 'Do you need anything else, John?'

'No, thanks. We'll be going out in a few minutes. I'm giving

Ian a look around the plant before the board meeting. Has everyone got the minutes?'

'They should have by now'. Darlene closed the door behind her. Macallister sipped at his coffee and then swore under his breath as he burned his lip. 'John, you remember our talk, about the whole process taking time. Well, this is part of the process. You have to take time to assess the situation and reach firm conclusions.'

'You mean, learn from our mistakes.'

'Not really. You haven't actually done anything yet. You've done some preliminary analysis and you aren't sure of the conclusions. Now what remains to be seen is whether the problem is with the conclusions themselves or the analysis that went into them. Don't worry about it. Wait until the meeting. How's Wendy?'

'Busy. She's working really hard at the moment. She's just opened another store and now she's got a new venture planned for Ottawa. I think it sounds really risky, but she's dead set on going ahead with it. She needs a rest. And then I've gone and asked my son to come and stay with us for Easter. Wendy get's on really well with my kids, but it's still a strain for her.'

'Why?'

'I was married before. She wasn't. It's hard to explain, but that's something that always lies between us. I suppose it's because I'm more sure of her than she is of me. And Keith and Cathy are a reminder of that.'

Macallister nodded. 'It all makes me glad I never married.'

Like a lot of men who are good at their jobs, Ian Macallister could sometimes be extraordinarily insensitive about personal matters. Hart was about to ask Ian about this girlfriend, but after that comment thought better of it. He looked at Macallister for a moment and then switched the topic of conversation back to the job at hand. 'Once we've finished the regular agenda, what I'm proposing is to call on Tony Leclerc the marketing director to present his ideas on how we should be approaching our markets. Once he is finished, I think we'll open the subject up for general discussion. I'd like to let the other directors have their say, and then call on you for comment. Does that sound all right?'

'Fine. I ought to add that my flight back is at seven o'clock, and I'll need to be back at the airport by 6:30.'

'We'll be finished well before then, I expect,' Hart said. 'All right. Bring your coffee, if you want, we'd better start the plant tour.'

They walked through the production area – moulding, assembly and printing – with Hart pointing out the various machines and explaining the processes involved. Macallister nodded, asking the occasional question but making no real comment. Hart felt that he was storing everything he had seen for later, getting ready to make comment and perhaps pass judgement some other time.

No doubt he had seen plenty of plants like this one before. As they came out of the print shop, Hart said, 'This must be one of the most interesting parts of your job. Getting to go around and see how different people do things differently in different businesses.'

'The different processes, you mean?' Macallister asked. 'Yes, it's fascinating seeing what different companies make and how they make it. Doing tours like this gives you quite a respect for technology and human ingenuity. We take so many of the things for granted in everyday life, without ever thinking about how they might be made – processes most people can't even imagine. And yet if companies like this one disappear, our quality of life would diminish.'

'If Wentworth Moulding closes it will mean the end of Western civilisation?'

'You know what I mean,' said Macallister. 'Go on, let's go face your board.'

Most of the directors and senior managers were already in the boardroom when Hart and Macallister arrived. Tony Leclerc was setting up an overhead projector and Shirley Easton was leafing through a small pile of transparencies. Tim Pringle was sitting at the far end of the table talking to Alan Mills and the assembly shop manager. Nick Moretti came in last of all and took the seat on Hart's left, facing the overhead projector screen.

'Right,' Hart said. 'Let's get started. First I want to introduce our guest. Ian Macallister of Strategy First in Montreal. Ian has, as you know, agreed to come in and help us take the pulse of the company and review our strategic ideas. This is an extraordinary meeting, and there is only one item of business, so I think we may as well dive straight in. Tony and Shirley are going to deliver a precis of our current marketing strategy, and then I'll invite Ian to comment. Tony, it's all yours.'

Tony Leclerc stood up beside the overhead projector and switched it on. 'I'm going to go through our current market, segment by segment. We have at present six identifiable segments. I'll describe them individually first, then we'll see how they all fit together.'

He laid the first transparency on the screen. 'Let's start with food. In terms of sales revenue this is the biggest single segment, although not by much, and it's also the one with the most steady customers – people like Conway Foods, who themselves sell in bulk through both large and small retail operations.'

'Then there's cosmetics. Now, nearly all our food customers are Canadian, while nearly all our cosmetics customers are in the States, am I right, Shirley?'

'Yes, that's right,' said Easton. 'We've concentrated on American companies using the differential of the lower-priced Canadian dollar as a selling point. In other words, we can sell the same product cheaper than our American rivals. Again it's steady business although there's some evolution as new products develop.'

'There are again several big cosmetics customers,' said Leclerc, 'big, that is, in terms of order size. Then we get a lot of small orders, sometimes repeats and sometimes not, from people who sell herbal preparations or small companies who make organic cosmetics. There's not much in that.'

'Except that market could grow,' said Easton.

'It could. Then there's fluid containers. Again, most of our customers are American companies. About 70 percent of our orders in this sector go south. Most of the customers here are chemical companies, and they, too, are steady customers. We take on large volumes on lower than normal margins. Jonestown Chemicals in Pennsylvania is our biggest customer by a long way; they make up probably 40 percent of our fluid container market. The rest are mostly smaller companies in Pennsylvania and New York. That's a historical thing; we had a rep in New York for a long time who used to work in chemicals, and he had very good contacts among the purchasing managers.

'Fourth is industrial products. This one's a bit different. Most of what we make goes to the automobile industry, and mostly in eastern Canada. The big three American makers and several other foreign makers have plants in southwestern Ontario, and we currently sell to all of them. It's a tricky market, because it's very dependent on the fortunes of the car market. When auto sales are up, we can be assured of steady, high-volume orders. When they're down, this sector takes a nose dive.

'Fifth is assembled products. We do a lot of small orders in this sector. An awful lot. We've two or three bigger customers who account for about 40 per cent of the segment.

'Last of all is sundries. This is a real mixed bag. We get regular orders from a business souvenir company in Hamilton that makes everything from letter-openers to boxes; there's a similar range of design, but everything is overprinted with something different. They're our biggest single customer. We have two large seasonal customers for Christmas decorations and related products. The remainder are typically small-volume orders. He looked up. 'As a matter of interest, sundry-product customers are responsible for an above average amount of work for the print shop.

'So, those are our six segments as we see them. They're necessarily broad, of course, and you can break some of them down into sub-segments if you like, but we like to keep our analyses simple. Now, Shirley has been updating our market intelligence reports, and I'm going to leave it up to her to describe what the market is doing.'

He sat down, leaning back in his chair, and Easton stood up. 'What's happening at the moment is that we've got two segments that, in sales terms, are growing, two which are declining, and two which are static. Food and cosmetics are definitely growing, and we see real opportunities there. We think that over the next five years we can grow our business in both these areas by anything up to 50 percent, and we're concentrating at the moment on trying to acquire new customers in these segments. My own belief is that in five years, these segments will represent the future of the company.

'Fluid containers and assembled products are holding steady. As you can see by this graph, the overall level of sales in each sector has remained consistent over the last three years, and we think it will continue to do so. However, as food and cosmetics continue to grow, it is recognised that though we'll make the same amount of money from both the fluid and assembled areas, that money will be less important to us.

'Industrial products and sundries, on the other hand, are declining. Industrial products, as Tony said, are in short-term decline because of the slump in the auto market, but could pick up again. I think if we can find a way of overcoming the short-term cyclical problems, there are opportunities in the industrial products market. At the moment, however, industrial products represent only about 10 percent of our total sales, the real sales figures are falling.

'We are weak in sundries. As you can see, this is our smallest segment. Why we're weak, I don't quite know. We lack specialist sales people in this area, and even if we hired more sales people, we doubt they could bring in enough sales to make the effort worthwhile. Sundries are not important to us at this time.

'The overall picture, then, is this. Our highest sales and our largest contributions to overall profit come from the food and cosmetics sectors which are also the sectors showing the highest growth rates. From a marketing perspective, we are well positioned to take advantage of growth in these markets. The major problem we have to solve is whether or not we as a company are equipped to take advantage of this growth.'

She sat down, not looking at either Macallister or Nick Moretti. Macallister himself was sitting with his elbows on the table, looking at the last transparency on the overhead screen. 'Could I see that one on the food segment again?' he asked.

Leclerc leaned forward and replaced the transparency. Macallister nodded. 'Growth averaging 10 percent a year over the last three years, and forecast to continue to do so. Contribution levels are well over company average. It all looks good so far. Now, you mentioned one customer, Conway Foods. Is Conway typical of customers in this segment?'

Leclerc nodded. 'A bit bigger, yes, but they order a typical range of products.'

'And are they typical of the sector in terms of things like price sensitivity, or quality and delivery times? And, are order volumes typical of the sector as well?'

'Hmm.' Leclerc looked at Shirley Easton, who shrugged. 'I'm not sure that they're typical in that respect, no. I meant that they are typical in terms of the kinds of products they order.'

'Then let me ask the same question of the manufacturing director,' said Macallister. 'Nick, are Conway Foods typical of companies in the food sector?'

Moretti, who had not been expecting the question, hesitated. 'Let me be painfully honest,' he said after a moment. 'Most of the time it doesn't matter, to me, if Conway Foods is the customer or not. An order comes through which specifies a customer's requirements in terms of total size, call-offs and deliveries, and I work to that. It could be Conway Foods or some other food product customer, or someone in a different segment altogether. I don't always see the difference. Now, in fact, because I like to keep on top of my job, I do know where the products are going. And I have to say that from my perspective there is no such thing as a "typical" food product customer. They're all different.'

'But hang on,' protested Leclerc, 'there are common features.'

'Tony, if you can see them, you're a better man than me. Of Conway Foods' last twenty orders, I'd say 15 of them have had radically different demands. High volume, low volume, fast deliveries, scheduled deliveries, some unprinted and some printed. Every possible permutation, they've had it.'

Before anyone else could speak Macallister said, 'And it follows, therefore, that if product specifications are all different, that contributions per product are all going to be different as well. You've got a figure there that gives typical contributions for the sector. But individual product contributions could literally be almost anywhere either side of that.'

'These are averages,' Leclerc said. 'You have to start from somewhere. I think it's fair to say that contributions from all products in the food segment are roughly the same.

'Sorry,' said Moretti. 'They're not. Run length and set-up times vary too widely for those averages to be anything but general figures. They tell us little about the individual products. Now I have to admit to being at fault here, because we don't keep records of things like set-up and run times for each individual order, so we can't tell you for certain what the contributions are for each product. But I can tell you that there is a very high level of variance. And the same level of variance can be found in the other five segments.'

'Couldn't we collect the information,' Tim Pringle said suddenly. 'We could use existing documents like worksheets and order sheets to find out what happened on individual orders over the last year. We can't go back any further than that.'

Macallister nodded. 'Hold that thought,' he said, 'because that's exactly what I'm going to ask someone to do. You can't keep talking about contributions in general terms. You've got to know what contribution each customer and each product is making to the total, if you're ever going to get any idea of who the good and less good customers are. You've got to look at all the costs of a product, including set-up time as well as run time. You may well find, for example, that when set-up times are added to low volume orders that you're not actually making any money. This chemical company, Jonestown, do they order from you once a year, or several times?'

'Several times,' said Leclerc. 'They place an order about once every two months.'

'So you pay set-up costs six times a year to get the same product volume. What does that do to your contributions?'

'But there are others who do order on an annual basis,' Easton said.

'Do you know who all of them are? We must find out. We must be able to review customers according to their behaviour toward Wentworth, not their behaviour toward their own product markets.'

Tony Leclerc leaned back in his chair. 'The thing that's been nagging me,' he said, 'is what do all these products and all our customers have in common? We start with a common denominator, that every company that comes to us wants something that can be injection-moulded. But what else is there? What else brings them to us?'

'Our reputation?' suggested Easton. 'Or quality, price, ability to deliver on schedule, reliability.'

Silence fell around the table.

'All customers,' continued Easton, 'have criteria which they are seeking to have fulfilled. They have quality demands, price demands, reliability demands and so forth.'

'Yes,' said Macallister. 'They all have a range of demands.

The question is, how do you win those orders? Why do you get the orders you get?'

'Because we do provide better quality or a lower price than the competition?' offered Easton.

'Ah,' said Tony Leclerc, leaning forward, and Hart could have sworn there was a light shining in his eye. 'But if we come back to the question of unifying factors, we find, what? We find that there aren't any. If we look at one customer, Conway Foods, we find according to what Dave Clarkson said last week that their main criteria is fast delivery time and meeting stringent hygiene standards. But if we look at Jonestown Chemicals, well, hygiene is hardly an issue. And fast delivery time is not as important as price, where they're very sensitive. We get orders from different customers in very different ways.'

Easton was scribbling rapidly on her notepad. 'So for our six market segments we should determine which factors win orders. Is that how we should review the answer to the question?'

'I think you need to revise a little more than that,' said Macallister. 'You have a tendency, like most executives, to use words like quality and reliability in a general way without defining what they mean, and that does not help when discussing your business. At the same time, you define your customers by what they do or what they put into a container. Does what your customers do really matter? And, more importantly, does it matter to manufacturing? To what extent is it a concern for you that Conway Foods is in the food business? The basic product you supply them is of injection-moulded plastic, the same as we do for other segments. What matters more is how many they want, when they want them, how quickly they want them, the price per unit and what conditions such as hygiene and so on have to be observed during the process.'

'Let's back up a minute,' said Leclerc. 'Sometimes it does matter what business a customer is in. Our industrial products market is affected by the nature of the auto industry, because demand rises and falls along with that market. Furthermore, customer contacts and technical issues involving a customer's processes are also industry-related. Furthermore, hygiene is more of an issue in some sectors than others.'

'Well, the first point you raise. Tony, is a behavioural issue,' interjected Easton quickly. 'It's a variable demand market, that's all we have to recognise. It doesn't matter if they're in the auto market or any other market. There'll be others that behave in a similar, if not the same, way. Look at the Christmas souvenirs we make in the sundries segment, that shows seasonal variations which changes the shape of demand.'

The two of them were beginning to argue back and forth and Hart leaned back for a moment, letting out his breath. This, he thought, this was getting them somewhere. Finally, there was some debate about the issues that mattered. But Macallister leaned forward and intervened.

'I don't want you to think I don't appreciate the work you've done so far,' he said to Easton and Leclerc. 'But I'm going to ask you to do several things, and then I want to set up another meeting with all of you again. First, I'd like someone to do what Tim suggested, take a sample of orders and go back over time and start trying to analyse exactly what contributions per order you are getting and how wide the variances are between orders.

'Then, and I want to particularly stress this for the next meeting, I want you to go over your customers again. By common agreement, select a number of customers that represent each of your six segments. If you are unsure that the chosen list represents the different dimensions within a segment then add other customers that reflect those other dimensions until you are satisfied. And this time, concentrate on trying to distinguish what customers require in terms of the business dimensions (for example, price and delivery speed) rather than the technical dimensions of their orders. To do this, you'll need to realise that there are two criteria by which you are judged in your markets.

'The first set of criteria are those that let you get into and stay in your chosen markets. They are, if you like, the table stakes.

They are criteria which mean that you are taken seriously by potential customers, customers who put you on their short-list when considering suppliers. These criteria are the *qualifiers*.

'Once you have qualified to be in the market, there is a second set of criteria. These are your winning hands, the criteria which mean you come out on top and win orders over the competition. These are the *order-winners*. Understanding both order-winners and qualifiers, how you get into a market and how you win orders in that market, is crucial to success.

'So, I need you now to examine your customers and identify the qualifiers and order-winners you need for each. And when that's done, let's look again at your markets.'

'And what will we do when we've done that?' Easton wanted to know.

Macallister laughed. 'Let's not run before we can walk. Let's see what our markets look like, before we decide how we're going to support their varying needs.'

Chapter 5

"How well do you understand your markets"

The morning sun was coming level across the rooftops, shining straight through the windows of Hart's office and blazing orange on the opposite wall. Hart finished his first cup of coffee and leaned back in his chair. The offices around him were quiet and only the muffled noises of men coming and going in the yard intruded on his thoughts.

He felt, in the aftermath of the meeting the previous week, that he had committed himself to a course. Tony Leclerc and Shirley Easton, he knew, still had doubts. But Hart himself believed firmly that they were now on the right track. Some simple analysis would confirm what they could already see, that segments were different to one another and, furthermore, that customers within one segment often sought different order-winners and qualifiers, as Macallister described them, and that these differences were not always relevant to the nature of the customers' own business.

Orders were won – and lost – for different reasons. They were beginning to think more about the customers themselves, and at the same time relate that new thinking to their own operations. What he had said to Wendy the previous weekend was increasingly true; he no longer thought of this as some sort of addendum to his job. This *was* his job; getting the right answers to the questions they were now posing was his principal executive role.

John Hart was, by the standards of most of his contemporaries, a successful man, yet he didn't think of himself as being in any way outstanding. His rise through the ranks in manufacturing in general and in Laurentian in particular was due to a steady competence – and a little good luck in being noticed – rather than any outstanding display of genius. He was good at what he did, but no more than that. For most people, that was enough. It had been enough for Hart for quite a few years as well, until he was given the job at Wentworth and came face to face, as if for the first time, with a wider world. What was good enough had changed because the task had changed.

However, it wasn't just the job. There was Wendy, too,

always a confident woman with many talents, but now on the verge of turning her business into a major success. The difference was that while his business was a reward for good service in the past and a vote of confidence in the future, he had done nothing to make it. Her business was a labour of love, begun by one person with an easel and a paintbrush and grown, at first, almost without thought of profit or expansion. She had made her business work by instinct, and now she was taking it further than either of them had ever dreamed was possible. Hart believed implicitly in her ability to succeed, and yet he worried about her.

There were his children as well; his son, Keith, was in the second year of a chemistry degree at Queens University in Kingston and beginning to think about a career after graduation, while his daughter, Cathy, would finish high school this June. Both still lived with their mother, and Hart did not see them, or think about them, as often as he might have. Yet they were always in the back of his mind, and the instinct to do something to make a better world for both of them was always there.

When he had accepted the job to run Wentworth he had been afraid that he might have even less time to think about these things, but the reverse had turned out to be true. For the first time in his life he was responsible for policy, for taking an entire organisation and making it see the world as he saw it; and yet at no previous time in his career had he been forced to give this moment any real thought. No one had ever asked him what his vision of the world was before they handed him the job. His wife and his children took on more significance now that he was confronted with the need to make up his mind, for in their problems and dilemmas he could sometimes see reflections of his own.

Something Macallister said kept ringing in his ears. '*Manufacturing creates wealth.*' Macallister had said it better, but he had believed in that premise for a very long time. When Hart first came to Wentworth he had seen the business in isolation; it was a company making products and selling them to other companies. Now his horizon was widening, just a little, just enough to see that a manufacturing business was more than just the sum of its output. A business was more than just an inventory list and a set of accounts. If there was nothing else, no one would bother trying to save a failing or stagnant business; let it go to the wall. Let another, better company, based perhaps in another country, fill the gap. Some manufacturing groups took exactly that perspective. But Laurentian, thank God, was not one of them. John Hart was not a sentimental man, but he was that morning full of immense gratitude, thankful that he had this job and thankful too that Mike Connors and Laurentian were willing to let him prove himself.

At a quarter to nine he poured himself a second cup of coffee and called Macallister in Montreal. 'Morning, Ian. I wasn't sure I'd get you in this early, but I thought I'd better try.'

'I've just walked in the door, as a matter of fact,' said Macallister. 'How are you? How is the company getting along?'

'Fine, fine. We've got an interesting new order from an existing company, and we're giving the specification a going over right now.'

'Trying to figure out if it's good business?'

'Well, no, trying to figure out if we can do it. I suppose it comes to the same thing in the end, doesn't it?'

'Mmm,' said Macallister. 'How's the analysis going? When will you be ready for me to get involved again?'

'We've talked through most of the market-related issues now, I think, and my marketing director is reviewing our customers using the fresh perspectives you suggested. I had a long discussion with Tony Leclerc and Shirley Easton on Monday, and I think we've sorted a few things out. They're now working on a fresh market review, which profiles customer demand by order size, quality standards, price sensitivity, delivery lead times and so on. Now I want to bring production into the picture, and I'm meeting with my manufacturing director this afternoon to discuss these perspectives and how we can link manufacturing and marketing at the corporate level. We've scheduled our monthly board meeting for next Thursday, that's the week before Easter. I want all parties to present their ideas on the market and argue it through. Can you be there? For psychological reasons I want some action on this before the holidays.'

'Let me check the diary.' There was a short pause and Macallister said, 'What time on Thursday?'

'We're meeting at 3:00 in the afternoon. Wait, I'd better check my own diary. Yes, three o'clock.'

'Sure, I can do that. I'll be there mid-morning,' explained Macallister, 'as I need to prepare for the discussion. Okay if I arrange directly with Alan and Nick for the data I need?'

'Sure. Anything else?'

'Space to work and a sandwich would help.'

'Okay, you've got it.'

There was another pause, and Macallister said, 'Finally, one last thing. What exactly are you expecting from this meeting, John?'

'A definition of the meaning of life, with a bit of luck. Failing that, at least a definition of where we are and where we're going. You asked me when you were down that first weekend, "How well do you understand your markets?" The answer is, not well, but I think we've made some real progress. I think we understand the problems, and we're ready to take a shot at finding some solutions.'

'Good,' said Macallister. 'I'll look forward to next Thursday, then. Until later.'

Hart put the telephone down slowly. He had hoped for something a bit more definite from Macallister, or at least something a bit more enthusiastic. His friend had sounded lukewarm, to say the least.

He put the matter out of his mind for the morning, because there was the usual routine to be done, including the morning tour of the plant. Keeping in touch was time-consuming but essential; most things which were important required time.

The short review of the plant was originally a throwback to his production days. But, Hart had come to realise that, used effectively, it gave him a real insight into a key aspect of the company while keeping him in touch with the people involved. That didn't mean allocating significant amounts of time. Regular contact and knowing what to look for kept the trade-offs more than favourable. Becoming remote was an easy condition to drift into. How had Macallister phrased it that first afternoon? 'Aquaplaning,' that was it. Even now it brought a smile to his lips. He was right. Some top executives' wheels never touch the tarmac. They get trapped in their own office suites and thus more and more manage from a distance.

He ate a quick lunch in the canteen with Shirley Easton and the Sales Office Manager, and then went back to his office to finish off the day's correspondence. He was just signing the last letter when Nick Moretti came in and sat down rather heavily on the sofa. He looked tired, and Hart said as much. 'When are you taking your holidays, Nick?'

'Not until June, not 'til the kids have finished school. It seems like a long time away, I can tell you.'

Hart felt he ought to say something sympathetic, about how the company was going through a few changes and how things would ease up once they were settled on their new course, but it all sounded trite. He decided to come straight to the point. 'Nick, following the discussions about markets and how we need to understand them better, particularly in terms of what our customers demand, we've been working on the problem. Following our general agreement on representative customers for each segment, Tony, Shirley Easton and I have already had one meeting about this, and Tony is now working on a new market review which will look more at what our customers actually demand from us, and less at the kinds of business they are in themselves. All of this is going to come up for detailed discussion at the next board meeting, but in the meantime I made a few notes from the conversation the three of us had. Although these are by no means final, they do give some idea of where the re-think is going. I'd like you to take a look at them and tell me what you think?'

'Right now?' said Moretti.

'Yes,' said Hart, handing over the single sheet of typed paper. 'I want your immediate reaction, as it were.'

The notes were little more than the brief summary he had given Macallister on the phone, and simply outlined the planned new segmentation. He wanted an immediate reaction because he was afraid his manufacturing director would, if given time to think the matter over, come up with objections. Nick Moretti was hardworking and conscientious, but his pessimism had to be overridden if any new idea was to have a chance. Catching Nick off guard was probably the best way of getting through to him. He was rewarded when, after five minutes, Moretti raised his head from the paper and said, 'I like it.'

'Go on.'

'Well, it makes sense to me. High volume and low volume, specific quality standards like hygiene, short or long delivery times; I mean, these are all the things I have to deal with. This is how *I* see customers. Conway Foods comes and says, we want x number of plastic trays for cook-chill food, I don't immediately think, oh, here's another order from the food sector. I think, here's an order for a lot of different products, all low-volume, all with a high quality specification, and probably all on just-in-time delivery, meaning we're going to have to hold finished goods inventory. I know Tony's over the moon about this order, and I agree it's a good piece of business. I mean, if it's good from the marketing point of view, it's got to be good for the company. But I'm going to have a few sleepless nights over this order, that's for sure. From my point of view it's going to be very difficult.'

He looked back at the piece of paper. 'But I'm getting off the subject. Yes, I think this kind of review makes sense. Would I be correct in saying that some parts of our present segments, like food products and cosmetics, may be virtually indistinguishable under this system?'

'I think so,' said Hart slowly. 'Don't you? You face the same kinds of problems in meeting some orders in both segments, and different problems when meeting other orders in both segments.'

'Pretty much. Hygiene standards for different food customers are, of course, similar. And I think short delivery lead times are, in general, more important for food than for cosmetics, but not in every case. Speed of delivery is a factor for some customers in both segments.'

'Are these fundamental differences, or differences of detail that you're describing?'

'From manufacturing's point of view, these differences are fundamental. Although the basic process of injection-moulding is the same no matter what we're making, the different demands placed on us by our different customers make these different businesses. The technology may be the same, but the segments are different from a business standpoint. Similarly, customers in the same segment may also be different. It's that critical difference I took away from the Macallister session. The business not technical dimension is the critical factor. In manufacturing we need to supply both the technical and business dimensions of an order. The latter is the one that doesn't get discussed. Thus, it makes sense to me to look at our markets this way. But then, I'm not a marketing man.'

'No, but based on your intuition,' Hart said, 'you're telling me that this separation makes sense to you. I'd rather our marketing concepts were not things which only marketing can understand. If you and Tony Leclerc can view our markets in the same way, then we're getting somewhere.'

Once again he was conscious of a distinct sense of the progress they were making. He really felt that he was coming to grips with the problem. 'What happens now?' asked Moretti.

'This is still basic, as I said,' Hart added. 'Tony is working on the details of the review now. Next he will present this new data at the board next Thursday, and then we, especially you, will get a chance to critique them and join in the debate. Ian Macallister will be there as well and will be giving us his comments. Tony's views are the initial input, but by no means represent the final statement on the subject. We have to agree on our markets and then proceed from there.'

'Okay,' said Moretti. 'I'll be interested to see what Tony has to say. If my views can help sort out our markets, then I'll be glad to give them.'

'Well, I'm hoping it will do more than that,' said Hart. 'I'm hoping it will sort out some of your production problems as well.'

Moretti laughed. 'I wouldn't go that far. None of this is going to make any difference to me, is it?'

For a second or two Hart just stared at him, feeling as though he had just bumped his head. 'I'm sorry,' he said finally.

'Look, boss,' said Moretti, obviously struggling for words. 'I think we may have got our wires crossed here. I'm trying to do my bit and help you and Tony work out a strategy for the company, and I take in what you say about needing to make the marketing concepts simple so we can all understand them. But there's nothing on this piece of paper that is going to make the production job any easier. We've still got to juggle schedules; we still have to worry about inventory of materials and finished stock; we still have all the problems we always have. Reassessing our markets isn't going to make any of those problems go away.'

And did you really think it would? was the unspoken addition to the last sentence. He looked at Moretti for a few seconds longer. 'Nick . . . . As I said, these are early days. You've got to take a certain amount on trust for the moment. Believe me, my ultimate strategy is to make the whole company, especially the manufacturing departments, better able to respond to the demands of the markets.'

'I understand that,' said Moretti. 'But the classic way is to get the marketing strategy sorted out first, isn't it, and then figure out how manufacturing needs to adapt to meet those needs? Like I said, I'm willing to put in my two cents, but I don't see anything that's going to affect me directly until that strategy is finally adopted.'

'So you think marketing strategy and manufacturing strategy ought to be kept completely separate?'

'Well, no, obviously you want to maintain communication. But in a marketing-led business it stands to reason that the marketing strategy comes first. And I thought that was what we were doing here,' he ended, defensively. 'I thought that formulating a new and better marketing strategy,' and he raised the piece of paper, 'was what this was all about.'

It was on the tip of Hart's tongue to say that he did not want to be marketing-driven but market-driven, and eventually to drive the market. But although this was indeed what he wanted, he did not know how to articulate the idea any further, and there was no point in trying to explain it now to Moretti. Instead, he said, 'It's very selfless of you, Nick, to lay down and let marketing walk over you, but I think you'd better start being a little more manufacturing oriented. I want you to do more than just put in your two cents at this meeting. I want you to challenge those initial views. Without input from you, we could, and probably would, be a long way from reality. We're going to have to test opinion to make sure we really understand our markets. Finally, I'm looking to you to explain what we can do well and what we do less well, so that when we come to agree on our markets, you can say what you would want to change and improve on the manufacturing side.'

'Okay,' said Moretti, and he got to his feet. 'But I can tell you that now; the same things I've always wanted. More machines, more operators, more production capacity. The problem from my end, John, is that these ideas are based on generalisations. I know that the differences between orders may appear to some as detail, and those details don't matter to marketing. But they're fundamental to me. I have to work with those details, all of them. Solving the problems, those details of quality, cost, delivery and scheduling create is what I spend my time doing.'

After Moretti left Hart sat down behind his desk and read slowly through the notes he had made. Moretti had not seemed at all pessimistic; on the contrary he had been quite cheerful. He had been genuinely enthusiastic about the new strategy because, to give him his due, he believed it would be good for the company. He simply did not believe it would make any difference to his problems in production. After taking two steps forward, he now felt he had taken at least one backwards.

Chapter 6

"Strategy resolution
is my #1 task"

Hart arrived home late feeling irritable. Wendy was sitting in the living room with her feet up, watching television. 'Keith rang,' she said, as Hart bent down to kiss her.

'Keith? What'd he want? Don't tell me he's broke again.'

'He might be, but he didn't say so. He wanted to know if he could spend Easter with us. His mother and sister have been invited to go to Florida with a friend, but he doesn't want to go.'

'He doesn't want to go to Florida? He must be crazy.'

'Maybe he wants to see you,' said Wendy. 'You haven't spent any time with him since last autumn.'

'Maybe he wants to touch me for a job at the factory this summer, that's more likely.' Hart sat down beside her on the sofa. 'What's this you're watching?'

'It's a travel programme, about Ottawa. You could call it research, I suppose. I thought it might give me some inspiration.'

'You're still thinking about Ottawa?' he said. 'Good grief, you haven't even got the London store open yet.'

'I believe it's called forward planning,' she said gravely. The programme came to an end, the credits rolling up the screen, and she reached for the remote. 'How'd your day go?'

'Quite well, until Nick Moretti informed me that marketing and manufacturing don't really have anything to do with each other. It's my fault; I should have made sure he was on side a long time ago. It's odd. He doesn't feel left out or ignored or anything, and he's quite happy to give his opinion where it's wanted. He just doesn't see how anything we're doing to the company is going to affect him, except possibly to increase his workload. He reckons more machines are the answer, and his task will be just more of the same. I outlined the procedure we would look to, but it fell on deaf ears.'

'Well, that is an inevitable consequence of success,' she said, as they got up and began to move through into the kitchen. 'The better you are, the more work you have to do.'

She was looking very tired; beneath her expertly made-up eyes, dark shadows spoke volumes. Hart said, 'I know it's none of my business. But are you over-extending yourself, in the business as well as the personal sense? You look like you could use a long break. Sit back and let the business take over for a bit, and give yourself some time.'

She smiled. 'I will when you will.'

'I'm being serious.'

'I know you are. It's kind of you to be concerned, but there may not be another opportunity like this. I've got the money in place, and I'm all ready to go. There's no reason why I shouldn't get the Ottawa shop going as soon as possible. I figure the risk is minimal, so why not go now?'

'*Is* the risk minimal? From what you said on the weekend, you're trying to go into quite a new line of business.'

'Not a new line of business,' she corrected. 'The new shop will be a smaller version of the Toronto gallery, selling more prints and fewer originals. The market will be different.'

'But that will be quite a different proposition to Chope Gallery in Toronto. You've already got three different businesses, that gallery, the print and frame shops and the picture restoration business. Aren't you spreading yourself a bit thin?'

She looked surprised. 'No, I don't think so. I'm just taking advantage of an opportunity.'

'I think you're taking on too much,' he said.

'It's all right,' she said, and there was a faint edge to her voice; she was, after all, very tired. 'I know what I'm doing.'

They drove to London on Saturday in Hart's Bronco, leaving far earlier than they needed, but Wendy was nervous that something might have been overlooked. While she and the manager of the new store went over the preparations for the opening, Hart walked around the mall. Most of the shops weren't open yet, and he virtually had the place to himself. He looked idly in the windows of a few shoe stores and toy stores, spotting in the latter a child's puzzle which came in a plastic box. The box had been made by Wentworth the previous autumn.

Smiling at this, he bought himself a cup of coffee at a kiosk from a waitress wearing pink and white rabbit ears. Everything was decked out for Easter; virtually every shop had some kind of Easter motif, and the candy stores had their windows stacked high with boxed Easter eggs. That reminded him that his son was coming to stay. How were they going to entertain him? Keith was 20 now, and presumably well past the time for Easter-egg hunts.

At 9:45 he went back to the shop. Several people were already waiting around that end of the mall and looking in the windows, intrigued as much by the sight of the table full of wine glasses and cheese trays, he suspected, as by the prints already hanging on the wall. He went in and found Wendy looking tense and a little pale. He gave her shoulders a squeeze. 'It'll be fine. Half the mall's already headed this way.'

'Thanks.' She looked across at Janet, the manager, and tapped her watch; ten minutes until the doors opened. Ten minutes until the trial began. A good opening was not vital to success, but experience had taught Wendy that a busy first day meant steady custom. If the first day was slow, you were liable to spend six months waiting and wondering if the site was going to pay. And, Hart knew, she had the Ottawa proposal in the back of her mind as well. Not for the first time, he thought she had come a long way from the painter and gallery owner he first met.

When the doors opened he picked up a glass of wine and moved across the room to stand and admire some of the framed prints; his role on these occasions was to stand and project a reassuring interest in the store and its contents. It was easy enough for the first hour or so, but by the time he had looked at each print five or six times he was beginning to get bored. He couldn't go home without Wendy, but he wondered how it would be received if he slipped out and had an early lunch downtown.

He was standing and pondering the possibility of a steak sandwich and a glass of beer when a tall woman in a red cardigan moved up beside him and said, 'Wendy tells me you're her husband. I'm Susan Clarkson.'

They shook hands. Susan Clarkson said with a smile, 'It's nice to see you here.'

'Oh? How so?'

'Well, we poor company wives usually have to trot around behind our husbands at business functions. It's nice to see a husband reciprocating the favour.'

As Wendy Hart could by no stretch of the imagination be described as a company wife, Hart felt justifiably annoyed. 'I don't mind in the least,' he said, looking around. 'I'm quite interested in painting, and I always think Wendy does a nice job on her shops. My only complaint is that when I come to these things I end up stuck in a shopping mall for hours on end.'

'Oh?'

'They're pretty dreary places, aren't they? I had a walk around this morning before the shops opened. I can't imagine why anyone would want to spend a Saturday in a place like this.'

The woman's smile diminished slightly. 'We like to think,' she said, 'that they come because we have created an ambience which appeals to them. We think most people like shopping in malls.'

'We?' said Hart blankly.

'Perhaps I should explain. I work for the company which manages this mall. That's how I know Wendy.'

Hart said nothing for a moment. Then he said, 'I'm sorry.'

'Why? You said what you thought. Sure, malls aren't for everybody, but that doesn't mean they're for nobody. So what do you do?'

'I run a moulding company in Hamilton. We make a whole range of plastic goods. The company is called Wentworth.'

'Oh, I've heard of you!' the woman exclaimed. 'In fact, you probably know my husband, David. He's CEO of a company called Conway Foods. You do business with them, don't you?'

Hart escaped as soon as he reasonably could, and told Wendy he was going out to get some lunch. She did not look pleased and looked even less so when he showed up again three hours later. Another couple of hours dragged by, and the shop shut; even then there was an hour to wait while Wendy added up the day's take, congratulated Janet and her staff on a job well done, and made sure they knew what was expected of them in the following week. Wendy was a stickler for detail in her business, and they did not leave until she was completely satisfied.

'Did it go all right?' Hart asked as they pulled out of the parking lot, finally heading for home.

'Good day. I think they'll do well. Janet's a pretty competent lady and always knows the right thing to say to people. Which is more than could be said for some. What did you say to my mall manager?'

'I told her I didn't like malls. How was I supposed to know she was a mall manager? Come to that, how was I supposed to know that she was the wife of one of my best customers?'

'You weren't, said Wendy quietly. 'But it wasn't exactly a help to me. If you'd rather stay home on these occasions, John, just tell me.'

The rest of the weekend was marked by a certain amount of tension in the Hart household. Monday morning found Hart back in his office, where things were also going from bad to worse. Tony Leclerc came in first thing, looking tired. 'John, I've spent most of the weekend going over our market segments. Can I give you a quick preview of my findings?'

'Go ahead.'

Leclerc had listed each segment. Within each two or three customers had been identified as being representative of their segment. Then he had listed the factors relevant to each segment under the headings 'order-winners' and 'qualifiers' as discussed earlier.

'It's interesting,' said Hart. 'This breakdown shows some clear differences between one part of our business and another.'

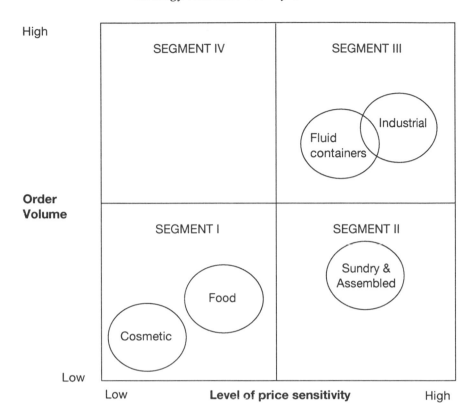

'Well, these are still early days,' said Leclerc, unconsciously echoing Hart's own words to Moretti. 'But I think simplicity is important here. In fact, I have placed the segments on this two-by-two matrix with high and low volume on the vertical axis and the level of price sensitivity on the horizontal. This diagram shows that the fluid container and industrial segments are high volume and are price sensitive while others, for example food, are on the low volume end of the continuum, but are relatively price insensitive. One thing such a breakdown will do is help us zero in on our best customers.'

'How are you defining best?' Hart asked. 'I thought some of the industrial products and containers customers had been our bread and butter for a long time. Jonestown Chemicals has placed a lot of orders with us over the years.'

'Yes, but it's never going to grow. Don't get me wrong; I think we need to keep supplying these people, but I think the strongest growth potential lies in this segment.' Leclerc was pointing to the low-volume/non-price sensitive segment. He added, 'I also think it's where we make most of our money.'

'Have you reviewed the data for a number of typical orders from these customers yet?' interrupted Hart. 'Without this there is no way we can know which are our "best" customers in terms of profitability.'

'I've not spoken to Alan Mills about this. Should I have?'

Hart shook his head. 'No, it's one of the next steps. We'll decide what to do following our next meeting.'

'Well,' continued Leclerc, 'we talked about qualifiers and order-winners. Now in this segment, qualifiers are things like cleanliness standards in the manufacturing process and meeting delivery dates. We can win orders by providing faster delivery, and by gaining a reputation for being flexible enough to meet the needs of the most demanding customers, at a suitable profit to ourselves. If we can provide just-in-time delivery and meet quality conformance requirements, we can expand our business with existing customers like Conway and get more customers in this segment.'

'These are the most difficult customers of all from the manufacturing standpoint,' Hart said. 'Nick Morretti is already having trouble handling the current volume of this kind of business.'

'So, what's the alternative?' Leclerc demanded. 'You've said it yourself, and Laurentian has said it as well, several times. We aren't increasing profits any more. We've got to take on more profitable business, get orders with higher margins. If we don't, we're stuck in this hole forever, as far as I can see.'

'Absolutely right,' Hart said sharply. 'However, the answer is to avoid overloading the production system with difficult orders so it can cope. If Moretti can't cope, quality and delivery times are going to go out the window, and our low-volume, high-profit customers are going to go with them.'

'So what is the answer?'

'I don't know,' Hart said. 'A week ago, I thought I knew. Now I'm not so sure.'

He could confess his doubts to Leclerc because the marketing director would be leaving soon, but to the rest of the directors and senior managers he had to appear confident and in control. His patience in this regard was tested several times that day. When the subject was broached to Alan Mills, he disagreed completely with Leclerc as to which segment was the most profitable; to him, some of the high-volume, long-standing customers in the industrial and fluid containers markets were more profitable, and the lower unit price was more than offset by the higher volume. He also pointed out that the cost of acquiring new customers was going to eat into Leclerc's proposed increased profits.

'Can you identify how much we earn from each customer, and what profit we make from each?' asked Hart.

'We can. It will take time, and I'm not sure how much manpower I can spare. Do you want me to start right away?'

'Wait until the board meeting.'

Hart's son telephoned at about 3:00. 'Hi, Dad. Are you picking me up from the coach station next Thursday?'

'Yes, of course. Did you ring me just to ask me that?'

'Well . . . I also wanted to talk to you. Dad, is there any chance of me getting a job with you this summer? I know I've only done two years of my degree, but I've learned a lot, and I really want to get some practical experience. What do you say?'

'Keith, I'm up to my eyes at the moment. We're in the middle of a major strategy review, and quite honestly, I don't know what the company will be doing or even for certain if there will be a company by the summer. Okay? I'll do what I can, but don't push me on this.'

'Yeah, okay, Dad. Sorry.'

'I'll see you on Thursday, Keith.'

He hung up, feeling guilty. The boy really was keen, there was no doubt, and at another time Hart would have been flattered that he wanted to get involved in his father's business. At the moment, an importunate twenty-year-old was the last thing Hart wanted to deal with.

However, he had to deal with an importunate company manager instead. At 3:20 he fielded a call from the purchasing manager of DKW, the chemical company in Albany, New York, and one of their fluid container customers. This one appeared to be even more price sensitive than most; he was demanding, without much ceremony, a price reduction of 4 percent on the next order.

'It can't be done, I'm afraid,' Hart said. 'We don't have much of a margin on these products as it is. Four percent is tantamount to charity.'

The purchasing manager had a New York accent which Hart found annoying. 'Well, something's got to give, somewhere,' he said. 'I gotta tell you, were looking around for other suppliers right now.'

'Fine,' said Hart. 'But if you think you can do better elsewhere, why come back to us?'

'Because we've had a pretty good relationship with you over the last few years. We've always found you to be reliable and reasonable.'

'But that's not worth 4 percent?' Hart said.

'Blood may be thicker than water,' the man from DKW said cryptically, 'but it ain't thicker than money. We're under pressure to cut costs all the time. Aren't all your customers under the same pressure? Do you tell them all to find another supplier? I can't believe that.'

'Give me 24 hours,' Hart said. 'My marketing director will get back to you.'

After all that it was almost a relief when Tim Pringle came in with the monthly manpower reports. Tim, unfailingly calm, sat and listened while Hart vented several of the things he would have liked to have said to the purchasing manager of DKW.

'Never mind,' said the personnel manager sympathetically. 'Easter's coming up. Take a nice long weekend and get away from it all. Are you and Wendy going anywhere?'

'No, my son is coming to stay with us. Tim, are you planning on taking any students for the summer? If so, I'll have him send you an application. I don't know if you can use him or not, but if you can, well . . . he's a good lad, and I think he's probably a good worker.'

'Thinking of founding an injection-moulding dynasty, are you?' Tim asked. 'Yes, we take three or four students each year, so tell him to go ahead. Well, that should be fun for you, having him stay.'

'I have to get through next week, first,' Hart said. 'Or rather, we all do. Tony is going to come into the board meeting and present his findings, which he is very excited about, and I'm increasingly afraid that my consultant friend is going to shoot them all down in flames.'

'Is he going to suggest something else in their place?'

'Ian, in his own words, doesn't tell people how to run their businesses. He tells people how to figure out for themselves how to run their businesses. The hell of it is, some of what Tony is saying makes me deeply uncomfortable. I keep telling myself that I'm reacting as Nick Moretti is reacting, and that it's because I've spent most of my career in production. I'm used to being down there with my nose to the wheel, and I'm not used to looking at the broad picture. But I can't help thinking that the bottom line in a business like this is not just "can marketing get the customers," but also, can production fill the orders, meet customer demands and make profits.'

'Seems reasonable,' said Pringle. 'It's like turning a telescope around and looking through it the other way. You do get a different view. So we're to get fireworks at the board meeting, eh? I wouldn't miss it.'

Somehow the fact that Tim wasn't taking the entire affair quite as seriously as he was made Hart feel slightly better. He finished off the afternoon thinking in odd moments of ways he could apologise to Wendy. He was just clearing his desk when Shirley Easton knocked at the office door. 'John? Sorry, are you on your way?'

'In a few minutes. Come on in. What's on your mind?'

'I just picked up your memo on DKW. Offhand, I'd say there's no way. To be honest, 4 percent on that kind of order is ridiculous.'

'Is there anything we can offer instead?'

'Hard to say. There's a basic quality standard we have to adhere to, but there's no demand for anything beyond that; we can't really offer a higher quality product. Delivery isn't an issue. I don't suppose there's anything that can be done about reducing costs . . . We might be able to persuade them to place larger orders so that we can do larger production runs. That might reduce our costs somewhat, but it would also have an impact on inventory. We'd have to check and see how much.'

'It seems to me that if we can genuinely manufacture larger production runs at a lower unit cost, that's an opportunity worth looking at. Tony thinks we ought to be going the opposite direction, looking for low-volume orders where the customer wants a high quality standard or very fast delivery and never mind the cost. What do you think?'

Shirley smiled. 'You want me to contradict my own boss?'

'You may as well know, if you haven't already guessed, that Tony is on his way to his own CEO's job, pretty well any day now. When he goes, you've got his job.'

Easton looked down at the carpet for the moment. 'Thanks, John. I'd been hoping.'

'I know you have. So don't worry about contradicting anyone. What do you think?'

There was a long silence, and Hart glanced surreptitiously at his watch; he was hoping to leave in time to stop at the florist's before it closed. 'I think,' said Easton finally, 'that what makes me most uncomfortable about all this segmentation and the idea that we can pick out one segment and focus on it is that things change. Markets change, faster all the time. Customers' needs change. Then there's the impact of product life cycles to consider. That's what we're facing with DKW now. We've been selling them the same products for a long time, and the downward pressure on price is starting to show. At the other end, where Tony wants to take us, those market segments are volatile and are probably going to get more so.'

'Some markets are stable, others are volatile,' Hart said. 'But Wentworth has lived with that for quite a few years.'

'And in the short run we've been successful. But in the long run we haven't, and it's the long run we're thinking about now, isn't it? We need to be looking ahead more than just six months or a year, we need to be thinking about two years, or three, or five, or all of these time frames at once. I don't want to criticise Tony, he's a smart guy, but I think he's got a pretty short-term outlook right now. He's thinking, what can we do to grab as much high-value business as possible now, and the answer is, go for the low-volume, high-price segments. But that's opportunistic, not strategic.'

'And what is strategic?'

'Some kind of plan we can work toward. Something that means we develop as a company. Look, I've criticised Tony, now I may as well criticise Nick too and have done with it. But all these ideas of going after more of this kind of business or that kind of business, these are all just snatched from the air. Our production side just isn't flexible enough to cope. We can't cut margins any more to help us win low-price orders, and we can't stretch our facilities enough to help win low-volume orders. It's a kind of a trap. We need a strategy that will help us cope with change, constant change, in the marketplace, yet we've got a system that seems to be cast in stone and can't respond to change when it comes.

'You're going to tell me I'm not being fair to Nick. I know I'm not. He does his best, and I'm glad I don't have his job. But, John, I don't think that the heart of our strategic problem lies in how we perceive the marketplace. I think it concerns ensuring that all our principal business functions directly meet the needs

91

of the marketplace. And I don't have a clue what we can do about it.'

Hart was late getting home, and as he had missed the florist, he arrived empty-handed. He walked into the house, feeling tongue-tied, wanting to apoligise but not really knowing what to say. Wendy was not there. When he turned on the answering machine there was a message from her saying that something had come up and she wouldn't be leaving the gallery until late, after nine at least. He made himself a sandwich for supper and ate it in front of the television, his mind somewhere else.

Chapter 7

"Strategy problems are complex and need to be resolved at the conceptual level"

The atmosphere at the start of the second meeting was considerably different from that of the first. Before, the directors and senior managers had not known what to expect; some had been looking forward to hearing what Macallister had to say, others had been indifferent. Now, all of them knew that Macallister had come to challenge them and was going to keep challenging them until they got things right. Macallister himself came in ahead of Hart, gave a general 'hello,' sat down, and began writing steadily on a notepad, not saying anything more to anyone.

Hart brought the meeting swiftly to order. 'Everyone knows what this is about. We've all been thinking about what Ian said, about order-winners and qualifiers, and we've been looking at ways of applying these concepts to our own company. Tony, do you want to start now?'

As he had said he would, Tony Leclerc had developed his ideas considerably since he had shown Hart his rough diagram the previous week. The same two-by-two went up on the overhead projector screen, but with a cautionary note that this was a very simplified version of the overall view of the market. Standing at the foot of the table, Leclerc proceeded to outline the original thinking which had led them to devise this segmentation in the first place. He went on to talk about consumer behaviour, and he talked about it with considerable knowledge; quite a lot of digging in the files and in Leclerc's own memory had gone into this part of the presentation. He could and did provide examples of every type of behaviour he discussed.

'We can see that there are several determining factors in customer behaviour, and most specifically, there are several determining factors which lead to Wentworth, rather than our competitors, getting orders. I've chosen to concentrate on the two which I feel are most important, order volume and price. Now, if we look at this graph, we can see there is an inverse relationship between volume and price. The higher the volume, the lower the price. This works, because our own setup costs are lower and we can afford to charge less per unit. But I don't think that these high-volume and, therefore, low-price orders are the most profitable ones. I think the real profit is to be made at the other end, with low volumes but correspondingly higher prices and higher profits per unit.

'What we've done here is, as Ian suggested, take sample orders from each of our six segments and analyse them. Our goal has been to find common factors which link these orders. What we've found is that segments exhibit quite different behaviour patterns and that we can group segments according to profitability. What I want to do now is suggest a prioritisation of market segments which will allow us to concentrate on the ones which are most profitable. You will notice that I am not concerned about volume; the issue here is profits, not sales.

'First, there are the low-volume customers who are relatively price insensitive. These are in our food and cosmetics segments. These customers also pay for higher quality standards and faster delivery. But that is exactly the point; they pay.

'Second, there are the lower-volume customers who require a lower quality specification and give longer delivery times by placing scheduled call-offs on our business. These customers correspondingly demand lower prices. They include a lot of sundry and assembled customers. I'm also including pharmaceutical customers here, who are part of the sundry sector. This is with the proviso that in some ways they resemble food customers in that they demand high product quality standards. However, in most other ways they behave much like the other sundry customers. Order volumes are typically higher in this sector than in food and cosmetics; you can see them plotted here, further up the vertical axis.

'Third and finally, there are the industrial products and fluid-container customers. I've ranked them last in importance, although I'm well aware that these customers have been our bread and butter for quite a few years. They place large orders, as I've said, at a comparatively low price and low profit per unit. I'm quite happy for us to continue taking these orders, and I'd like to see these customers continuing to form the foundation of the business. I want to build on the foundation, however, by expanding into the first segment.. The third segment gives us sales; the first segment gives us profits.'

He looked up the table at Hart as he switched off the overhead projector. As the noise of the fan died away, Leclerc said, 'That's how I see things and I'm quite aware that this is very much a marketing perspective.'

'You've done a good job of putting it across,' Hart said, and he saw Macallister nod slightly. 'I think we all recognise the amount of work you've put into this presentation. Okay, who has any comments to make?'

Alan Mills leaned forward, tapping his pen on the papers in front of him. 'Tony, what figures have you used to calculate the profitability of these segments?'

Leclerc sat down and poured himself a cup of coffee from the pot on the table. 'I used last year's figures, breaking down different product ranges according to sales and profit per order. I used a pretty random sample of about 60 orders, which I figured gave a proper range, some from each of the six market segments.'

'So you're talking about profit per order,' Mills said. 'Is that based on standard costs?'

'Yes, I used your costing figures.'

'Nick?' said Hart. 'Any comments?'

'One of the biggest factors is set-up time,' said Moretti. 'Typically, it takes from three to six hours to complete a set-up, regardless of run length. So, the longer the order, the better the productive to non-productive ratio.'

'Alan,' said Hart, 'set-up costs are treated as overhead. Correct?'

Mills nodded. 'That's Group procedure.'

Macallister raised one eyebrow, but said nothing. 'I think I've cut setup costs about as far as they can be cut,' Moretti said bluntly. 'If we concentrate on Tony's first segment of low-volume orders, our *overall* costs, not just our product costs, are going to skyrocket. Can we charge enough to justify them?'

Leclerc, not surprisingly, was looking resigned to the form and nature of manufacturing's counter agreements. 'Nick. Can you see no way, no way at all, that we can be more flexible, more responsive to customer needs? We're talking to a customer now, DKW Chemicals, where we already have a wafer-thin profit margin, and they want to cut the price by 4 per cent. The longer we hang onto a customer, producing the same product, the more the downward pressure on price builds. We need to get customers who aren't constantly pressing us on price, who will allow us room to make profits, but in exchange we've got to be able to provide them with what they want – quality, technical support and delivery performance.'

'You're going to mention Conway Foods, any minute now,' Moretti said with a knowing smile. 'Though I can't tell you whether an order like theirs is actually more profitable or not, I can tell you that orders of that kind cost me a great deal of non-productive time and present a scheduling nightmare. I wish I could guarantee that I could go on and on meeting a variety of complex, short-run, fast-turnaround orders without compromising costs and delivery. But eventually, something is going to give. And the thing is, with this kind of order, there isn't time to rectify mistakes when they do occur. We've already had that problem recently with, if I'm not mistaken, Conway Foods themselves.'

'So what do you need?' asked Hart.

'More focus,' said Moretti. 'More direction. I agree with Tony that I'd like to see us emphasise one market segment. The question is, which one? It's a sad truth that flexibility for marketing means more problems for production. When I first saw the notes you made, Tony, I said to myself, "Yes, I like the feel of this. This is beginning to make some sense of the problems I face. I can see different production problems emerging from different types of orders." But what you're saying now is that you want to move in the opposite direction from where I would ideally like to go.'

Deadlock, Hart said to himself. It was pretty much what he had increasingly foreseen over the last week. It was time to see if Ian Macallister could break the logjam. 'Ian? You've heard the different viewpoints. What do you think?'

Macallister stirred in his chair, looking for a moment at the notes he had been making. He ran a hand through his hair. 'Where shall I start? This wasn't a fringe benefit that was advertised when I joined the consulting profession. Travel the world, meet interesting people, challenge their thinking and test their tolerance levels.' There was a laugh around the table, in which even Tony Leclerc joined. 'Right. You seem to have divided yourself into two rival camps. One sees the key to success lying in greater flexibility, the other sees it in more structure and long-term stability. You're waiting for me to tell you which is right.'

'It would sure be nice if you did,' said Tim Pringle.

Macallister smiled. 'I'm not here to help review your conclusions, but your reasoning. Okay, let's look at the stability party first. Nick. Why are you so convinced that nothing can be done to improve profitability from the production end of the business?

'I didn't say there was nothing that could be done,' said Moretti. 'I've said a good many times, in this room and elsewhere, that we can become more profitable if we can increase our overall production capacity. But we can't do that until we have formulated a strategy, and the whole rationale for increasing producing capacity and production itself hinges on a marketing strategy which tells us what business we want.'

'Marketing strategy?' said Macallister. 'Do you believe all of this just concerns a marketing strategy? What about the rest of the business? Are you content to let production and other functions respond to the demands marketing places on them? Obviously you aren't; you're worried, quite rightly I would say, that the pressures already placed on the system are straining it. But you're describing strategy like it's a club sandwich, with all sorts of different layers held together by a toothpick.

In most companies, CEOs require functional executives to provide functional statements on strategy. And, because the essential integrative nature of strategy is ignored in this process, the distinct and independent layering referred to earlier is the outcome. In fact, the nearest these functional strategies become to be integrated is that they sit side by side, layer by layer, in the corporate strategy binder. Integration is not provided if, in fact, it was ever intended. Hence, many functional strategies are characterised by their reactive natures rather than being an essential part of the corporate debate leading to agreed strategic direction. Without this, for instance, companies ignore the fact that just as markets have an internal dimension in that they place demands within a company, manufacturing has an external dimension in terms of its ability to support the order-winners and qualifiers of chosen markets.

'This problem is made worse when companies seek to resolve strategic approaches by reviewing companies as a whole. This is typically undertaken by overlaying corporate diversity with generic strategies. Niche, low cost, core competence-type arguments are seductive in their apparent offering. The promise of uniformity is appealing to those with the task of developing strategies for businesses which are typified by difference not similarity. In fact, such approaches purport to bring about a corporate similarity which, though desirable, is inherently not available. The alternative, therefore, is to recognise difference and develop multi-strategies to address these separate needs. However, while Tony has recognised that difference exists from his function's perspective, other functions have yet to provide similar insights as essential inputs to the corporate debate. Already, we appear to have arrived at an either/or position without adequate understanding of all the issues involved.

'The first step yet to be accomplished is to gain a clear understanding of the various markets in which you compete. Without this, functional strategies cannot be developed. With this you can then set about designing a production response to meet the needs of your various markets.

'So far, what you've got is a one-dimensional input into strategy; you've considered marketing's view, but you haven't looked at the manufacturing response. And I'm bound to say from my own experience, this is the pattern which most companies follow. The outcomes are disconnected strategies the shortcomings of which it is argued, can be overcome by adopting, for example, a flexible manufacturing response. The logic, therefore, of such proposals is that the diversity of markets can be met by apparently all-embracing developments embodied in phrases such as 'flexible manufacturing'. But flexibility, for example, can not only be different points on a continuum but also comprises more than one continuum. Specifying a company's market needs is the key step. Configuring the manufacturing system then follows.'

'Can you tell us more about how we ought to configure our system?' Moretti asked.

'If you'll allow me I'll come back to that issue when we know more about the nature of the demand to be placed on it. But I do have something I wish to show you. Nick, as well as each of you, has identified capacity as a constraint. It is hampering the opportunity to grow. Also, Group has rejected your request for investment to increase capacity on two counts. First, your profit levels are too low and secondly, they are not clear on where you believe you are going.

'I mentioned earlier that developing a strategy for a business takes several months. You need the time to think things through and also to identify what data you need to collect in order to test opinion and gain fresh insights. In parallel to Tony's analysis, I also looked at further data this morning on some of the same orders he used. The purpose of this is to provide additional perspective on the same issue about markets, as well as provide essential input regarding capacity and its use. If I could use your overhead projector, Tony, I will show you the results.'

Everyone sat looking intently at the table. The most remarkable thing about the data was that there was little pattern to it. 'I found,' Macallister said to the quiet room 'that reviewing actual contribution per hour for the selected orders gives some different, and in some instances very different, insights. The range is not only very wide, but those contribution levels at the low end will undoubtedly be loss-making once the overhead has been taken into account. For example, this order from Jonestown Chemicals is one in question where you would undoubtedly have suffered a loss.

'In addition, when you review the different markets here, most segments are not consistent within themselves. Thus, these two orders within the cosmetic sector show much higher contribution per hour figures than the others. Also, the levels of contribution may, and often do, differ between orders from the same customer. As long as you look at market segments in general you will end up developing market views based, as far as manufacturing is concerned, on generalities. In the same way, you also need to check that there is consistency between orders from the same customer.'

Leclerc said nothing. 'You've put all food and cosmetic customers into the same segment,' Macallister went on. 'But do all food and cosmetics companies behave the same way?'

'No,' said Leclerc, 'of course there are some whose behaviour more closely matches other segments. I was speaking in general terms, you're right, but that was for the purpose of illustration. I propose to look at every customer, now and in the future, to see where it fits in the segmentation scheme.'

'Sorry,' Macallister said slowly, 'I haven't made myself clear. The questions that need to be answered are: Do all customers within a segment reflect a similar set of order-winners and qualifiers. Then the same question needs to be addressed to each customer: Do all orders from the same customers have the same order-winners and qualifiers? For example, do any companies place, say, a high-volume order where price in an order-winner and also place orders which are low volume and requiring fast delivery? If so, where do you place the company?'

'We could,' said Shirley Easton, jumping in for the first time, 'place them where the majority of their business is, or where their core business is.'

'No,' said Tim Pringle. 'Aren't you then getting back to defining customers by their business, rather than by their behaviour?'

'Or,' said Easton, 'we could apply the segmentation to each type of order, not to each customer.'

Macallister spread his hands. 'Why not?'

'Where would that get us?' asked Alan Mills.

'Closer to an understanding of the needs of the market,' said Macallister, 'and further from assumptions which stem from generalities. That will allow a viable and appropriate production response. It will also allow you to look for the specific kinds of orders you want, not the kinds of segments or customers you want. Which is more important to you, Nick? Different kinds of segments, different kinds of customers or different kinds of orders?'

'I presume that's a rhetorical question,' said Moretti.

'It was. As you will deduce, these perspectives bring a new dimension to the market debate. From the marketing standpoints, separation by industry type (such as food and cosmetics) is an important dimension in understanding and approaching customers. For manufacturing, such separation is often of no consequence. What is of consequence to manufacturing is the importance of different order-winners such as price, delivery speed and so on. These are the dimensions which secured the order and which your business needs to provide. Your initial analyses have illustrated a common feature of markets, that of difference.

'Like others, the question you need to ask is, how should you cope with difference? Many do it by finding the lowest common denominator. In this way, they have some broad and roomy definitions into which the wide expanse of difference, future changes and even the unexpected can, with a little trimming and folding, be accommodated. But that isn't the way of dealing with the problem, it's a way of obscuring it.

'Forgive me for lecturing you. I know that all of you are trying to keep your strategy as simple as possible, and that's laudable. As far as I am aware there is no virtue in complexity. But there's a key difference between being simple and being simplistic.

'Strategy problems are complex. To resolve them a company needs concepts to give insights and to help choose between outcomes, a recognition that it is a problem requiring an intellectual resolution and hard work. And, that's a difficult trio. However, these will enable you to gain essential insights. For, strategy is not a process leading to generalisations. Nothing would be further from the truth. It's a distillation process with the task of identifying the very essence of what comprises a business. In particular, as your business is serving different markets, your strategic process and outcomes need to reflect those differences. The typical strategic response to the complex needs of a business is to create a general approach which tries to meet all needs in the same way, leading ultimately to a general strategic statement. Nothing could be further from what is actually required. The strategy process must provide essential direction, and you cannot cope with differences by glossing over them. And, the path from complexity to simplicity has its origins in hard work.'

Chapter 8

"Manufacturing's response must mirror market differences"

Toward the end of the meeting Alan Mills brought up the subject of analysis. 'I really think we should get back to this question of costs and related contributions for each order. Do we want to check that out?'

'You need to analyse several dimensions,' Macallister responded. 'For all the customers representing each segment, we need to check a number of factors. The analysis I gave earlier included actual direct labour costs, but only standard costs for materials including packaging. You also need to collect actual material and packaging costs. Only in that way will we be able to establish actual contribution per machine hour. Within direct costs you should include the set up costs related to a change-over. Also, if there are any other actual direct or variable costs, such as transport, these have to be introduced.

'Then, you also need to identify other data relating to the order-winners and qualifiers specifically associated with the segments those orders represent. For example, customer lead times relating to delivery speed, meeting schedules relating to delivery reliability and customer returns/complaints relating to quality. I'll go through all of this with you to identify clearly related data.

'This analysis will lead to a way of testing your opinions on what wins orders and it will also highlight similarities and dissimilarities within what you currently perceive as your markets. This will help review your markets, verify what wins orders, and it will ultimately enable you to confirm a strategy based upon a more complete understanding.

'So, yes, I think you should prepare a full report on all these things. When we meet next, we can start re-looking at segments, both in marketing and manufacturing terms. Identify which orders require which production tasks and associated capabilities. Establish that view of segmentation, and you will be on the right road.'

'Who's going to prepare the report?' Leclerc wanted to know. 'Me, or Nick?'

'Who pulls it altogether is probably not so important. But the perspectives need to be shared and then analyses based on actual data, not on standard costs or opinions of what happens in terms of other criteria. Someone does, however, need to coordinate all this and bring it together.'

Shirley Easton said, 'I'll do it.'

'Have you got the time?'

'I'll make the time. I want to do this, it's important.'

'It's the most important thing you can do at this stage,' Macallister said. 'You've got to be sure of your information before you make decisions. If I might add a word of advice, don't decide anything, not yet. Wait. Build in some thinking time.'

When the meeting was over, Hart walked with Macallister back to his office. 'Do you want a lift to the airport?'

'Don't worry, I can get a cab. You'll want to get home.'

'I also need to talk to you.'

They drove to the airport, making nothing more than small talk while Hart concentrated on his driving in rush hour. As they pulled into the airport, Hart said, 'Do we have time for a drink?'

'Sure. Come on, I'll stand you a beer.'

In the airport lounge Macallister ordered two beers and raised his to the light. 'Cheers. And cheer up. It didn't go so badly.'

'You think so?' Hart said dubiously. 'All the time you were talking I sat and thought how little we really know about our own business.'

'That's not true. You're too busy, and you're too close to the problem. If it was all that simple,' Macallister said with a wry smile, 'there wouldn't be any need for guys like me, and I'd be out of a job. You tried out a few ideas, I came in and gave you a critique of them. Now you're going away to test the ideas with analysis. You're making progress.'

'I'm glad you think so.'

'Seriously. You're on the right track as far as markets are concerned. Eventually, you will need to translate that market understanding into a response from within the company. I think you'll find that the analysis turns up some interesting points and provides key insights as well. You'll get there.'

'But how *can* we make that translation? Seriously, Ian, I'm unsure how we can solve this problem. Moretti said to me some time ago that he saw all this as being essentially a marketing problem, and that his job was just to react to what marketing needs. He sees that as part of being a marketing-driven company.'

'Yes. He feels that anything which is good for marketing has to be good for the company, but that things which are good for the company are not necessarily good for production. That will only change as he gets more involved in the problem; I call it "commitment through understanding." I think the closer you get to the reality of how manufacturing supports chosen markets and the more you can eliminate ambivalence about what it is you are actually doing, the happier Moretti will be. Again, the results of the analysis will give you some essential insights and help you see the business with more clarity.

'But he's got to understand,' continued Macallister, 'they've all got to understand – that analysis of markets is undertaken to identify problems and raise issues. But markets don't provide solutions, unfortunately. The solution to the problems has to come from within the company. Start looking at the company, John, and start thinking about what you can change about the company to help solve problems and address issues. And think about this; just as markets are often defined in general terms, so companies are often organised along general lines. Once you start defining specific market problems, then you have to look at finding specific company solutions. Don't be afraid to think in radical terms.'

'How about raising it to the ground and starting over?' Hart said. 'Yes, all right. Shall I call you in a couple of weeks, and we can discuss progress?'

'Sure. Or call me anytime if something unexpected crops up.' Macallister drained his glass. 'Right, I'd better get going. Take it easy, John. My best to Wendy.'

It was nearly 8:00 by the time Hart got home. Wendy was in the living room sitting on the sofa with papers spread out in front of her on the coffee table. She was working steadily with her laptop computer and a calculator. She looked up when Hart walked in and dropped his briefcase. 'Hi! I made some dinner; yours is in the oven. How did it go?'

'Not well,' said Hart. He summed up the meeting in a few sentences. 'Ian thinks it went okay. Apparently all this is part of the learning process.'

'Well, he is the expert. I think he's probably right. Trial and error is one of the best ways to learn.'

'We can't afford errors,' Hart said sharply. 'Not at this level. We've *got* to get this right. A wrong decision now could prove a disaster.'

Wendy looked at him for a moment. 'And yet, you've got to take some risks. I don't know where this exercise is leading you and the company, but I can guess that it will involve some fairly radical changes. How can it do anything else? As far as I can see, you're doing all the conventional manufacturing things exactly right but performance is lagging. What you're going to need to succeed is a break with convention.'

Hart looked at his wife. 'How do you know we're doing all the conventional manufacturing things?'

'Common sense,' said Wendy. 'Coupled with an article by your Mr. Macallister which I ran across in a management magazine last week. We keep them in the foyer outside my office along with the arts reviews to convince customers that we're serious and businesslike, but I can't say I ever read one until now. It was a good article. If you weren't already getting it from the horse's mouth, I'd suggest you read it.'

'It obviously impressed you.'

'He speaks, and writes common sense. And common sense says that in this case, if you're doing everything right and you still aren't succeeeding, then go back to basics and be prepared to try something even though it might at first appear to be contrary to conventional wisdom. The problem, of course, is that any attempt at growth is fraught with risks. You see how tense I get when I'm in the process of opening up a new store or trying something new, and I know I'm probably pretty difficult to live with right now. But, it's got to be done. Growth has risks; not growing brings with it certainty. Certainty of stagnation and long, slow decline, if you're lucky.'

'Why do you do it?' he asked her. 'Why go on? What's the end result supposed to be? Will you go on opening shops or galleries *ad infinitum*?'

He had never asked her that question before; it was a subject they had never really discussed. When they were first married the gallery was already a successful concern, and the first fledgling shop had just been opened. Since then he had watched with pride and a certain sense of astonishment as she went from strength to strength. Her toughness and acumen never ceased to amaze him. It was only now that he was beginning to wonder what it was all for. She saved the document she was writing and switched off the computer, leaning back and looking at him.

'I go on because it makes me happy,' she said. 'I like what I'm doing. I like the challenge, and success is its own reward. I won't keep opening shops forever; I don't know what I'll do in the end. But whatever I do, I'll make it a success, and I'll keep building on what I've got. I started off as an artist, but I've grown to like the challenges of running a business. So, I suppose the answer is that I'll go on as long as I find value in what I do.'

'So the element of risk is important to you.'

'Well, it's a given. No pain, no gain, as they say.'

'What about the consequences of failure? The money, the people who depend on you and look to you for leadership and direction; the jobs that hang on your decisions? And it gets worse as you grow, the proportions get bigger and the consequences more serious.'

'John,' she said softly. 'You're having an attack of nerves

because things didn't go well at the meeting. But it was only a meeting. You haven't actually done anything yet, you haven't committed yourself to anything. You're in the planning stage, and you still have a lot of things to work through. That's all.'

'No, it isn't all. It's beginning to come home to me just how much I've taken on with this job. I want to succeed, just as badly as you do, but I know what's at stake. It isn't just a game, or something at which I want to succeed for the sake of success.'

'And you think I treat it like a game?' she said quietly.

'I'm not sure what you're doing any longer. This whole Ottawa thing, for example, it doesn't make any sense. Why you're doing it, I don't know. Almost for the hell of it.'

She stood up. 'For the hell of it? Have you been listening to anything I've said? Do you really think I don't take this seriously?'

'No,' he said finally, 'I don't think that. I'm sorry. I'm tired, and I've not had a good day. Forget what I've said.'

'It's not going to be that easy,' said Wendy.

That was the start of an Easter weekend which seemed to go from bad to worse. Keith arrived at the Toronto coach station on Friday morning, and Hart drove him back to the house. Wendy was friendly to him, asking him about the courses he was taking and life at university, but she said very little to Hart.

Hart and Keith went for a walk across the fields on Saturday morning. The snow was gone now, and the fields were very wet with mud that clung to their boots. 'Did you get a chance to ask anyone about me getting a job?' Keith asked.

'Yes. Have you got a résumé? Well write one, and send it to the personnel manager. His name's Pringle, Tim Pringle. I'll give you the address when we get back to the house.'

'Thanks, Dad. It'll mean a lot. It's important when you graduate that you've already got some experience in business, isn't it? I mean, it makes you more marketable.'

'Are you sure you want to go into business? You're studying

to be a chemist, doesn't research or teaching interest you?'

'No, I want to go into business. I'm thinking of going to Western once I graduate, and doing my MBA. I mean it's not just about making money, is it? Being successful in business helps create wealth, and that's good for the country.'

'Is that what they teach you in university nowadays?' Hart asked. 'Things have certainly changed. When I was an undergraduate, we all had long hair and were calling for the death of capitalism.'

'That wasn't very realistic,' said Keith, with devastating simplicity. Hart smiled. 'No, it wasn't, certainly not in my case. All right, manager-to-be, I've got a problem for you to solve. I need to make some changes in the way the business is run. On the one hand, I'm under pressure to be more flexible and adapt to what my customers want. On the other hand, there's a limit to the changes I can make, and it's better for the business if we remain fixed and focused on the pressures of the short term versus the desirability of the long term. What should I do?'

They walked to the end of the field, turned, and began to walk back to the house. 'That's hard,' Keith said at length.

'Yes, it is.'

'Tell me some more,' responded Keith.

So, the rest of the walk was taken up with discussing particular issues and business in general.

That was probably the only light note of the weekend. Having Keith stay was not, under the circumstances, the best thing to have done. Hart thought, not for the first time, that his son was younger than his years; he had an almost puppydog eagerness that could at times be endearing but now, strained as things were, was simply annoying. Wendy felt it even worse; several times, Hart, watching her, could see her almost biting her lip in an effort to avoid snapping at the boy. It was not Keith's fault; he was simply eager to please. So they bore it all without speaking.

Hart drove Keith back to the coach station on Easter Monday morning, and, feeling suddenly guilty, he urged his son to make sure he sent his résumé to Tim Pringle. 'It would be good to have you around for the summer. We don't see enough of each other, and it would be a good chance to get caught up.'

'I'd like to work with you, Dad. I think it would be really great.' Hart stayed to watch the Greyhound leave, then drove rather slowly back to the house.

There he found Wendy looking at commercial real estate listings in Ottawa. She had circled a property in the city centre near Parliament Hill which had a lease coming due in two weeks.

'Are you going to see it?'

'I'm going to call about it tomorrow. It's on offer for a good price, and it's the location I want. I can't afford to miss the opportunity.'

'And you really think you can branch out in yet another direction and make it work?'

She turned around. 'John. Just because it's different doesn't mean it's wrong, okay? For me, the key is to look at how things can be different and work, not how much they differ from past experience or expected norms.'

'But you're not just going into a new market. You're going to do business in quite a different way.'

'And what on earth is wrong with that? Different markets demand different methods. John, I really do know what I'm doing.'

He was tired and nervous, and so was she; so when he said something he should not have said, she did not forgive him easily. The argument which ensued seemed to go on for a long time, and it took most of the rest of the day before the atmosphere calmed sufficiently for them to be able to talk normally. Around midnight they sat together on the living room sofa, and he put his arm, tentatively, around her shoulders.

'I won't bite,' she said. 'At least, not now.'

'It seems almost futile to apologise. I do believe you know what you are doing. But I can't help worrying about you, in much the same way as I presume you are worrying about me.'

'Whatever made you think I was worrying about you?' she said calmly. 'I don't think you have a serious problem. There's nothing wrong with your business that some analysis and a little reflection won't cure. I have every confidence that you will sort things out. Frankly, John, I didn't marry you so I could sit and worry about your job.'

That seemed to kill the conversation. 'I think I'll go to bed,' Hart said finally. 'This may be a four-day week, but it's going to seem a lot longer. Are you coming?'

'I'll sit up for a while,' she said. She gave him a smile as he got up, which looked rather forced. 'I haven't had much time on my own this weekend. I'd like to just sit and think for a bit.'

'Okay,' he said quietly. 'Don't be late.' As he went upstairs he glanced down and saw that she was looking at the real estate listings again, and that her finger was resting on the property she had circled earlier. She was completely absorbed and barely heard him when he said good night.

Chapter 9

"Digging the detail"

The telephone rang and Hart, deep in the middle of a report, lifted the receiver and said rather absently, 'Hart speaking.'

'John,' said Darlene, 'I've got Mike Connors on the line.'

Hart sat up hurriedly; Connors was the last person he felt like talking to this morning. Two weeks had now passed since the infamous board meeting before Easter, and he still had made very little in the way of progress. 'Put him through.'

'John,' said Connors a moment later. 'Good morning. How are you all doing up there?'

'Fine, fine,' Hart said energetically. 'We're looking at a couple of new orders, one of which could be quite big. Things are looking up.' He winced slightly, hoping he did not sound too insincere.

Apparently he did not. 'Good going,' said Connors. 'I'm pleased to hear it. John, I'm sorry about this, and I'm aware I'm going to put a crimp in your operations, but I'm taking Tony Leclerc away from you. There's a nice little printing operation down in Pennsylvania which needs an energetic marketing man to give it a boost, and I reckon Tony's our man.'

'Well, I'm sorry to lose him, but I'm happy to see him get his chance. When does he go?'

'I think end of May, if you can spare him by then. He might want a bit of time off between jobs, too, he'll have to see about getting moved. I know it's short notice, but I think we've got to move quickly on this one.'

'I think Tony will be delighted, whatever the notice. Have you told him yet?'

'No, I'm going to talk to him just after I've finished talking to you. Now, have you got any ideas on who you want to replace him?'

'I've got a replacement right here. Shirley Easton has been Tony's deputy for about two years now. She knows the company and its markets as well as Tony, and she's deeply involved in our present strategy exercise. Under the circumstances, I don't want to waste time and lose momentum breaking in a new director, and I think Shirley is right for the job.'

'Yeah, I know her. She's good. Okay, you've got it. You can tell her she's got the job, and I'll have personnel write and confirm the post and her new salary, and follow up on all of the contract details. How's the new strategy going, John?'

'Well . . . We've had to go back to square one, it seems, and do a lot more analysis. Apparently some of our assumptions about the company and its markets weren't very well founded. It looks like its going to take a little more time than we anticipated.'

He heard Connors chuckle on the other end of the phone. 'I started off in advertising quite a few years ago now, and I remember we had a saying. "Digging the detail." It's kind of like reading the manual when you can't figure out how to fix your car; it's often the last thing you think of doing.'

Hart, who did not particularly appreciate being reduced to the status of an aphorism, said, 'It's not that it's the last thing we thought of doing, but that the time to do analysis is rather hard to come by. We've reluctantly decided that it will have to take a high priority, and just get on with it.'

'So what are you analysing?'

'Two things. Why do we get the orders we get, and which of those orders make the most significant contributions? We think if we can sort out those dimensions we can see where our best market opportunities lie.'

'Sounds good. You hang in there, John, and keep plugging. We've got every confidence in you down here.'

Hart replaced the receiver, thinking that Connors' last remark was the sort of thing football owners said about coaches just before they fired them. Well, it was unlikely to come to that – yet. But there was no doubt in his mind that he was now under the gun.

Shirley Easton was a woman in her late thirties who had decided rather later in life than most that she wanted to be in business. It was a hard decision for a recently married woman with a small son, but she had made it, going back to university to get a business degree and then deciding for reasons, which were not entirely clear even to herself, to look at the engineering and manufacturing sectors for jobs. While her colleagues went off to financial services, accounting, IT and consulting firms, Shirley Easton had sent her CV to the personnel director of the Laurentian group and asked for a job.

She still thought on occasion that they hired her because they were so surprised at getting an application from a woman, and in fact she was partly right. Mike Connors, then personnel director, had approved her initial appointment on the grounds that her direct approach indicated toughness of mind. After three years as a marketing executive with an engineering firm in Quebec, she had applied for and got the job of development manager at Wentworth. 'Selling plastic bottles?' asked her husband incredulously. 'You want to move back to Ontario to take a job selling *plastic bottles*?'

'They're containers, not bottles,' she said. 'And if you want me to start telling lawyer jokes, just keep going.' They had moved back to Ontario, and it had been a success; her husband was now practising law in a small firm in St. Catherines, and she, it appeared, was about to realise a dream; she was about to become marketing director, with full responsibility for marketing strategy and for helping take the company into the future.

Sitting at her desk and smoking her favourite brand of menthol cigarette, Shirley frowned. Her sympathy for the plight of John Hart, which had increased steadily ever since he had taken over as CEO, moved up another notch. No one in business or at business school had taught her how to face the problem on the immediate horizon. Not the present problem, the question of analysing customers, finding out what moved them, and learning from which customers the company derived its profits; not this problem, but the next one she could see looming ahead, the question of what they were going to do to support the changing needs of the market. She had considerably more sympathy for the plight of Nick Moretti than did her erstwhile superior, but then Shirley Easton's first degree was in engineering and she knew as well as Moretti the size of the problems which had to be faced.

On the previous day Moretti had provided her with a list which he felt represented the full range of orders he had to deal with for each of the designated markets in terms of size, delivery speed and other criteria. Easton had looked up each order and found out the other necessary details and had compiled a list. Now armed with this and a number of questions scribbled down on a note pad by her right hand, she put a clean sheet of paper on her blotter and picked up the telephone. Right, she thought to herself. Let's find out what our customers really think of us.

The first call was to an old friend, Jim Wing, a fellow business school alumnus who was now working for a chemical company in Burlington. Jim picked up the telephone on the third ring. 'Shirley. How are you this bright sunny morning? Gee, isn't it great outside? This is the sort of day I can't stand being in the office, you know? I'd rather be home digging up the garden. Anyway, what can I do for you?'

Shirley Easton seldom paid much attention to weather; it was either snowing out, or it wasn't. 'Nothing much, Jim, just a social call. I'm doing a bit of research on customers, you know, the usual kind of thing, and I need to ask you a couple of questions.'

'Sure, shoot.'

'Basically it's this: why did your company pick Wentworth over the competition in the first place, and having done so, why do you stick with us?'

There was a shout of laughter on the other end of the phone. 'Nothing simple, the woman says, just the meaning of life. Why did we pick you over the competition. It was all so long ago.'

'It was last year, Jim.'

'Exactly. Well, let's see. There was a personal thing, of

course. I knew you and knew I could do business with you, that was a big factor.'

'Yeah, but what about the product? What sold you on that?'

'I'd have a real hard time breaking it down to individual benefits, you know? I mean, I looked at a package and compared that to the package offered by other companies, and yours came out best on points. You're going to ask me how I did my scoring. Well . . . the usual things. Price, of course, but timely delivery, quality and low reject rates are essential, and then, as I said, the fact I could do business with you. I knew if I had a problem, I could come to you and get it sorted out.'

Shirley smiled. 'For old time's sake?'

'Absolutely. How is that husband of yours?'

'He's fine. And why do you stick with us?'

'What? Oh, why do we keep coming back for more? Because you've met all our demands so far, I suppose, and we're satisfied. That being said, we also suffer from a commercial inertia against switching. There's a time and cost increment involved in finding another supplier, and so far you've given us no incentive to do so. Sorry this is so simple, I suspect you were looking for more complicated reasons.'

'No. No, I'm not sure I was. Jim, I'm looking at the moment at a particular order which you placed with us early this year, for some 120-litre containers. The order number was BT2120, if it helps you remember, and you wanted 10,000 units, which we duly delivered. Do you remember the one?'

'Vaguely.'

'What particular criteria did you set for that order? What prompted you to use us as a supplier?'

She knew the answer even before it was spoken. 'The main reason we used you was because we were already using you as a supplier. Criteria for the order? If I remember right, we were looking for a relatively fast delivery time on that one, because we were working against a short deadline ourselves, for our own customer. Low rejects would also have been important. But the basic criteria are no different from those we set for all our orders.'

Easton frowned. 'All right, let's look at it from another angle. Suppose that had been the first order you placed with us, and you didn't know us. Are the criteria we would have had to satisfy for that order the same as the ones you mentioned above?'

'Hypothetically speaking, I suppose the answer is yes. Is any of this helping?'

'Yes. Yes, it's a start, anyway. Thanks for your help, Jim.'

'Any time.'

The next two people on the list proved to be out of their offices. The fourth call was to a food company in Massachusetts, a comparatively new customer. Here she was on less familiar ground; she did not know anyone at Excalibur and had not been involved with the original order. She was aware that there had been problems with them in the past. The purchasing manager was off sick, she was informed, but his deputy would speak to her.

The deputy was a soft-spoken New Englander. 'Wentworth Mouldings? Yes, you make containers for our soft-cheese range. I can't think why we don't use you for some of our other products. What kind of range do you make?'

'A pretty wide range, really. Would you like me to send you some samples?'

'Do that.' They talked about the matter for a few minutes before Easton steered the conversation around to the reason for her call. She explained in an offhand manner that she was doing some general research and asked her question. 'Why did you choose us over the competition in the first place, and why do you continue to use us?'

'Hmmm.' There was a long pause. 'I'd say we chose you because we were favourably impressed with the end product, and with the sales rep we dealt with. He convinced us that you could meet all our specifications on quality, delivery, and of course, price. As I'm sure you're aware, one of our greatest requirements is cleanliness.'

'But weren't other companies able to offer you the same thing?'

'To be honest, a number of them didn't seem to appreciate the extent of our need for cleanliness. We weren't sure they would take it seriously. Your company and several others did. After that, it was all a matter of price.'

'What about delivery? You mentioned that.'

'Well, of course we need the product delivered on time,' said the deputy purchasing manager.

'But you've had problems with us since – batches delivered where the hygiene standard was not met. Haven't you been tempted to switch to another supplier?'

The deputy purchasing manager sounded amused. 'Well, that's rather an odd question for a marketer to be asking. As a matter of fact we have, and we have issued dire threats to your rep that if the problem happens again we may well switch. But, I should tell you in fairness that we are not at all sure we will get better quality from another supplier, and you have been good about rushing replacement orders to us. There are switching costs to think about as well. All in all, we'd prefer you simply got your house in order and supplied us on a zero-defect basis.'

'Sure,' said Easton. 'As you probably guessed, part of this review is to help prioritise our future actions, so many thanks for the feedback.'

She was still doodling on her blank sheet of paper a few minutes later when there was a knock on the door. Tony Leclerc came in with a sheaf of papers in his hand. 'How's it going?'

'It isn't, yet. I decided to do a little sampling and phone around to some of our customers. But apart from the usual problem of half of them being unavailable at any given moment, I don't think I'm getting any real data. A lot of gripes, a few backhanded compliments, but nothing on which we can hang any conclusions.'

Leclerc sat down on one corner of her desk. 'The problem is, they know us. They'd rather chat or complain than give us any rational feedback. Would John go for our using an outside research company to get some data?'

'It'd be expensive. Anyway, we're looking for patterns of behaviour, not the reasons that explain it, at least, not yet. I feel the key is to undertake the analyses ourselves. A third party would not understand the background context essential to the questions and insights we need.'

Leclerc nodded. 'I agree. Let's push on with it. On another tack. When you get a moment, could you look at these new specifications from Conway Foods? They've changed their minds about what they want again.'

Shirley Easton sighed and reached for the papers. 'Better do it now and get it over with.'

It was late in the afternoon before she had time to consider the analysis once more. Closing the door and sitting down with a cigarette and a fresh cup of coffee, she picked up her piece of paper once more and began writing. Occasionally she paused for long moments to think, once or twice getting up to go and stand at the office window and look out over the plant as the sun began going down behind it.

The quick conversations she had had that morning had not been entirely wasted; they had confirmed a few pieces of her thinking. First, of the many criteria which seemed to go into deciding whether Wentworth could compete for orders and whether it could win them, some were related mainly to the manufacturing process, and some were not. Price, quality conformance, and delivery reliability – that is, getting the product made and finished on time – were all things which were directly dependent on the production side of the business. On the other hand, some of the factors people had mentioned, such as the company's own marketing and sales ability and its status as an existing supplier, were only tangentially related to the manufacturing side of the business, if at all.

It was while she was getting her second cup of coffee that she decided that there was a third, intermediate, category of factors which were dependent on the manufacturing side, but not specific to it. Product design was obviously one; the other was distribution – the other half of the delivery factor, where the finished product was moved from the factory to the customer. The difference between delivery and distribution might not be readily apparent to the customer, but from an internal perspective it was important.

So, there were three categories of factors: manufacturing-specific, manufacturing-related, but not specific, and non-manufacturing related. Best take them in order.

Under the heading of manufacturing-specific factors she wrote 'price' and then paused for a moment. What did people mean when they said price was important? Price had always been a factor in the mind of the customer. But, in some markets, price did not work in the same way as in others. In some the price had to be in the ball park while in others, the central issue was price level. On some orders we have, the margins are much higher than for others. Like most criteria, therefore, price could be either a qualifier or order-winner depending upon the order.

Then there was delivery. Delivery had two dimensions, 'delivery reliability' and 'delivery speed'. Delivery reliability was a qualifier for most customers. Wentworth wouldn't be able to compete for orders unless it met, and continued to meet, delivery schedules on a regular basis. Short customer lead times were, in turn, part of delivery speed. Customers set delivery lead times according to their own needs and being able to deliver faster than competitors and thereby meet a customer's needs might be the order-winner, whereas being able to deliver on-time would work as a qualifier.

Shirley paused recognising that she had never debated these key differences before. And yet they were not only critical in themselves but more so when applied to markets. Without this clarity, how could any company understand its markets sufficiently? How could they identify the differences that typically exist in a company's markets? She returned to the list. Next was that uncomfortable word 'quality'. Twenty years had passed since the Japanese manufacturing giants had made quality a central issue in manufacturing and had forced the rest of the world to do likewise in order to keep up. Now quality was on everyone's lips; everyone knew quality was important. Everyone's expectations on quality had changed, but not everyone could agree on a definition.

In Wentworth's case, quality was purely and simply meeting the product specification agreed to with the customer. If a customer wanted a product to be 100 percent clean, then it had to be 100 percent clean; if he wanted it to be a particular shade of blue, then no other shade of blue would do. The ability to meet the specification was paramount. In fact, the Japanese had changed customers' expectations on quality to the point where in most markets it was no longer an order-winner, but a qualifier.

Shirley looked up. The file on Conway Foods lying on the corner of the desk caught her eye. Then another thought struck her, and she quickly wrote 'demand increases' at the bottom of the list. There were a lot of products where demand either increased steadily over time or fluctuated according to seasonal or market variations. Ability to cope with suddenly increased demand could well be an order-winner in some markets. Conway Foods had come back to Wentworth because they believed the company was able to meet their own sudden need for many more products. What had they called it at the board meeting a couple of months ago? 'Flexible production.' Well, this was certainly one aspect of flexibility.

That finished the manufacturing-specific factors. She looked at the next heading, manufacturing-related, but not specific, and wrote down two more headings, 'design' and 'distribution.'

There were a couple of aspects to design. One was quality. Not all quality issues stemmed directly from the manufacturing process, and the design of the product, as well as the process, was important. She drew a thick black line between the headings 'quality' and 'design' and stared at it for a moment before attaching an arrowhead to each end of the line. The other aspect was time. In her last company, design and development lead times had been much longer than they were at Wentworth, and orders had been won and lost on how long it would take to get a new product to market. Given that their own customers could win orders by the fast introduction of one of its products, then Wentworth's ability to provide packaging quickly could well be an order-winner. It took time to design and order a mould for a new product, and customers rarely planned ahead. Most wanted the product yesterday and didn't seem to understand that Wentworth couldn't produce moulds like rabbits out of a hat. Pushing that lead-time down could be important. It could win orders.

Then there was distribution. Customers wanted products delivered on time. This was more important for some than for others, particularly in terms of requiring an exact time. Distribution was a vital factor in meeting this criterion. In a lot of cases, of course, it was also vital to keep inventory and holding costs down.

It was getting dark outside. She looked at the final section, non-manufacturing-related factors. There were a number of factors which could be considered, but she doubted if most of them applied to this particular industry. The company didn't have a brand name; customers attached their own brands to the product. After-sales support was limited to following up deliveries, ensuring customers were satisfied and moving as fast as possible to rectify matters if they weren't. She wrote down 'customer care?', doubtfully. One factor here was the level of ability and effort from the marketing and sales functions. The ability of the sales reps to persuade customers to buy from Wentworth was part of what secured the deal – an order-winner so obvious that it seemed in danger of being overlooked. And then for repeat business, there was the factor of being an existing supplier. Experience, coupled with the comments she had heard that morning, told her that people tended to stick with existing suppliers even if not 100 percent satisfied; they preferred the devil they knew. Having won the first order, there was a greater chance that the company would go on winning them from the same customer.

She dropped her pen and leaned back. That seemed to cover all of the important factors. Now, how do we apply them to the customers? All the products of course were customised in that they met the required specifications of a customer. In fact, the product belonged to the customer. However, that did not make them 'specials' from a manufacturing viewpoint. They were obviously standard products as invariably they were ordered many times over the length of their life cycle. So, looking at segments through customers led directly to a review of the products they required and, in turn, to the orders for these they placed. Once this was understood, then she recognised that she could build back up to an understanding of the market. Now it was becoming clear why this level of detail was necessary. Only then could consistency within an industrial sector and/or between customers within a sector be checked. Only then could segments be developed where the task of supporting similar order-winners and qualifiers would lead to giving functions a consistent strategic task. It was all beginning to fall into place. The question was how to start.

She looked at the list of factors and thought about calling Tony for a second opinion and was vaguely surprised to find it was after 7:00. She rang home, talked to her husband for a moment and learned that her son was upstairs doing his homework. All was well. She looked back at her list again.

Suppose the sample Moretti had given her was roughly representative. She was sure it was. After the last meeting Nick had begun to take this project very seriously and had put a lot of thought into trying to define the order parameters within which he worked. Now, each product needed to be weighted against each possible order-winner. She would give each order a total of 100 points, as Macallister had intimated, to be divided between each factor as appropriate. Qualifiers also needed to be identified, but not as part of the weighting procedure. Hmm? She made a mental note to ask Macallister to explain that.

Now, the task was to identify relevant order winners and qualifiers both for now and in the future. In my early attempts, thought Easton, it may help me to look at historical perform-ance, going back one or two years, and see if things have changed. When that's finished, we can look forward and try to make some assumptions about what will happen in the future.

Where will the data come from? Well, every company file has copies of specifications and sales contracts. When read care-fully, these tell what factors the company thought were impor-tant. If necessary, I can ring some of these people and ask specific questions like 'Which is more important to you, delivery speed or price?' The task then is to spread the 100 points across relevant criteria. What had Macallister said when she spoke to him on this. 'Beware of spreading the points evenly across a range of criteria. The purpose of this part of a market review was to bring about clearer insights by identifying levels of importance. And secondly, the outcomes are statements of magnitude not exactness. Sixty points, for example, signals a factor to be much much more important than one weighted at 10 points.'

She drew a deep breath and looked at the first product on her list. CA1436 was the product reference. Her earlier thoughts had given her inspiration. She had picked an eight ounce con-tainer which, by chance, was an identical product sold to two different customers in the food industry. 'Trust me to find an exception. Well,' she thought, 'this should be the acid test; will both companies score similarly?'

Wentworth had been supplying both companies for about three years. The reps' notes which accompanied the original contracts noted that both companies had come to Wentworth because of dissatisfaction with their previous mutual supplier. There had been complaints about unreliable delivery, failure to respond to customer lead times, and about the fact that the supplier didn't seem concerned by the customer's complaints. There had been an attitude problem. As was usual with pro-ducts for the food industry, there were fairly strict hygiene

Criteria	Dewhurst and Pearsons			Snacklines		
	current year	next year	three years out	current year	next year	three years out
Existing supplier	20	20	20	20	15	10
Delivery – reliability	Q	QQ	QQ	Q	QQ	QQ
– speed	45	40	40	40	35	35
Quality conformance	Q	QQ	QQ	Q	QQ	QQ
Price	35	40	40	40	50	55
Marketing and sales	–	–	–	–	–	–

requirements. She also noted, reading through, that Snacklines was becoming more price sensitive than Dewhurst and Pearsons and had negotiated a price reduction last year; they had been given it on the assumption that the company would increase its overall business with Wentworth. A quick file check showed that the company's volumes had changed little in terms of annual totals or call-offs.

So there it was. Quality, delivery speed, delivery reliability, marketing and sales, being an existing supplier and price were all part of the original purchase decision. Quality and price were standard factors at this point, while delivery and marketing and sales seemed to be crucial to winning both orders. For the first year, two years ago, she assigned 30 points to delivery speed, 20 points to both delivery reliability and marketing and sales, with 15 points each to quality and price. For the second year, she hesitated for a moment, then reduced marketing and sales to 0 and added 20 points to price and 10 points under the category of being an existing supplier. She pondered again over the last; being an existing supplier had helped them win other orders from this company, but had it helped them keep this one? The answer was, probably, yes; the price reduction and new product negotiations showed that the company was interested in sticking with Wentworth for this product.

Now, let's do it for real. Current year with next year and the two after that as being the relevant future time periods. She pondered, checked her thinking and finally agreed in her own mind the following weightings relating to these two customers.

She leaned back and ran a hand through her hair, and after a moment got up to go out and make some fresh coffee. She was astounded to see by the clock above the coffee machine that it was after 9:00. She was equally astonished to see John Hart's office door open and Hart himself appear in the doorway.

'Shirley? I didn't realise you were still here. I heard a noise and thought I'd better investigate. I've had the OPP around again bending my ear about security on the premises, and I thought perhaps we had a burglar.'

'No, just a fool who doesn't know when it's time to go home. You're late tonight as well.'

'Oh, just a lot of things to clear up. My wife is working late in Toronto, so there's not much point in going home.'

'If I don't get out of here soon, I'm not going to have a home to go to,' said Easton. 'Want a cup of coffee?'

'Yes, why not? What are you working on that keeps you so late?'

Easton grimaced. 'Analysis. For the S-word project, you know?' She looked Hart straight in the face. 'I'm doing a pretty half-baked job of it, too. When you see what I've done, you may want to start advertising for a marketing director.'

'Nobody's expecting a thesis on the subject,' Hart said. 'I just want something with some numbers attached to it that gives us a starting point to debate and from there to go forward. Come on. Get your coffee and come and tell me what you've got so far.'

Chapter 10

"Strategy is a long haul"

Several weeks had gone by and the subject of Ottawa had disappeared from all conversation. Wendy no longer sat and looked at real estate brochures, nor did she contemplate expanding her art business any further. But no new topics of conversation seemed to have emerged to fill the hole. When Hart asked her how the new store was gong she said simply, 'Fine,' and would not elaborate. Meanwhile, she continued to look more and more tired, and the effort of not smoking was often a visible one. Once, while having a drink with friends, she had, without a word, gone to the cigarette machine and come back with a pack. She had then sat and played with the unopened pack throughout the evening and left them on the table when they went home.

She was coming home later and later from Toronto, and usually going straight to bed when she arrived. Hart wanted desparately to get her to tell him what was wrong, why she was driving herself like this, but he always held back because he knew that he himself was part of the problem.

It's not that I'm not supportive, he told himself as he drove to work, watching the sunlit lake glide by on his left and the office buildings and smokestacks of Hamilton appear ahead. Probably it's the opposite problem; I'm interfering and it isn't wanted. I rammed my views down her throat, and now she doesn't trust me any more, not where the business is concerned. She'll go ahead now and do whatever she wants to do without telling me.

That thought hurt. They had often joked in the past that their's was a business marriage, and he sometimes teased her by saying that she had proposed to him while running a spreadsheet package. They had come together in the first place through talking about their jobs, sharing problems and sometimes even putting their heads together to work out solutions. They had criticised each other's decisions before, many times. But it had never been like this.

Before him opened the gates of Wentworth, and there were the usual figures, Dave Kochner standing and shooting the breeze with the night shift foreman, Judy Salucci getting out of her car – she had finally been prevailed upon to take a loan from the company and was now driving a rather smart little Toyota – and Alan Mills, arriving at the office rather earlier than usual. He saw Tim Pringle's car there as well. Contract and pay negotiations were due to start that afternoon, and Pringle, in particular, had a long three weeks in front of him.

He parked the Bronco, got out, said the usual good mornings and went inside to look quickly at the mail and then go off to spend 45 minutes with Pringle, checking their strategy in advance of the first pay negotiation session. There were half a dozen telephone messages waiting for him when he got back to his office, and then he set off on his tour of the plant. He missed Nick Moretti in the moulding shop, but Nick came up to him in the assembly area, displeasure weighing on his heavy features, and said, 'What's all this about splitting up the plant?'

Hart stared at him. 'Nick, what are you talking about? Who's said anything about splitting up the plant?'

'Easton. This analysis exercise is supposed to be aimed at defining our markets and reaching a better strategy. Going around talking about re-organising the whole plant is going a bit far, in my book.'

'I don't think she can have meant it, Nick. She is looking at products, yes, and costs, but I don't think we meant her to be looking at processes. There's not much we can do with those, is there?'

'There sure isn't. We're running the whole shop about as economically as is possible, assuming Tim doesn't give the farm away in the pay negotiations, and any talk about trying to tinker with the organisation is out of order as far as I'm concerned.'

'Well, maybe she was pulling your leg. I'll check with Shirley. Any problems this morning?'

'Apart from smart-aleck development managers, no,' said Moretti. He was still scowling, but he looked slightly relieved as well, and Hart felt a twinge of annoyance with Shirley Easton. He was still annoyed when he got back to his office, and picked up the phone and dialled her extension straight away.

'Morning, John. I'm glad you called, I wanted to talk to you.'

'The feeling is mutual. What did you say to our manufacturing director to wind him up so badly?'

There was an exasperated noise on the other end of the phone. 'It was an innocent remark. Nothing was meant or intended. Alan and I were looking at costs, and I went down late yesterday to get some figures from him on actual labour hours per order. When he gave them to me I glanced at them, and there was such an obvious anomaly that I made a crack about him running two different plants, that maybe he ought to be running two different operations. It was just a . . . oh, never mind.'

'Well, he took it seriously. What was this anomaly that was so striking?'

'Just the difference in total labour hours for low-volume versus high-volume products. John, I think I'm just about finished. I think we need to talk about some of the things I've found.'

'All right.' Hart looked at his desk diary which seemed to be solid black ink. 'It had better be today. The pay negotiation sessions should finish at 4:00. My office at half past? Tell Tony, and I think Nick had better be there as well, if only to soothe his ruffled feathers.'

The pay negotiation session came and went. These negotations were always delicate, and nobody was expecting a quick solution. On the other hand, everyone was extremely amiable and, so far as Hart could see, both sides seemed to be taking the other seriously, and Tim Pringle managed the meeting in an exemplary fashion. That was a good start, and Hart breathed a sigh of relief when it was over. 'Well done, Tim. I think I can leave the rest of it in your capable hands. I'll drop in from time to time to show the flag. Call me if you need someone to come around and play the heavy.'

'Don't think we'll need it. They sound intractable, but they'll come around. Most people like working here, and most are satisfied with the terms on offer. The brinkmanship will only last until we all get bored, and I reckon that will happen by middle of next week. Look for a signing by next Friday, I'd say.'

'On our terms or theirs?'

'Ours, of course.' Pringle grinned. 'What's next for you? I gather the results of Shirley's analysis are coming in.'

'Yes, I'm just off to hear what she has to say. Then I reckon we'd better get Ian Macallister back in here to add to the debate. What did you think of Ian, Tim?'

'I thought he talked sense. He avoided giving a straight answer to any question, but then I suppose all consultants do that. But I liked him.'

Back in his office, Hart just had time to make a quick phone call to Wendy. She was on the other line, the secretary said, and did he want to hold? He held on until there was a knock at the door and put the receiver down reluctantly as Leclerc and Easton came in.

'I've asked Darlene to bring us all some very strong coffee,' said Leclerc. 'Smelling salts will also be available on request. On second thoughts, we should have got some anyway, for Nick.'

'It's all very well for you,' said Easton, sitting down. 'You're bugging out and leaving us to face the consequences. I'm the one who has to hang on and take the flak.' The development manager was clearly nervous. Darlene came and put a tray with cups of coffee on the low table next to the desk, and Nick Moretti came in rather warily just as she went out, closing the door behind her.

'Right,' Hart said. 'We haven't got a lot of time. Shirley, what have you got to show us?'

'I've done two different things which relate to each other. The first thing was to take the orders sample which Nick provided and group the orders along the lines Ian Macallister suggested and which we've been talking about, by size of order volume. As you can see by this table, I've grouped them by market type. The sample orders are listed down the left side of the chart by product code. Then I've listed the volume for the last three orders. The determining factor for volume as you can see in this column is average standard hours per production run. Can you see, Nick?'

'Yes. What's this one, CX1101?'

'It's a cosmetics product, for a moisturising cream I think. We also part assemble them. We made them for Glorielle Essences in Montreal, until they dropped us last year.'

No one said anything to that. Easton went on, 'Across the top I've listed the different order-winners and qualifiers that I think relate to each product. I've grouped them again, as you can see into three categories, manufacturing-specific, manufacturing-related, but not specific, and not related to manufacturing, again in line with Macallister's advice. These headings underneath are the specific categories like price, quality, etc.

'Now, what I did to start with was to analyse which factors led to our winning the order for a product in the first place and then why we received the repeat business. Going backwards was not part of what was required and, with some products, the initial order was too far back to be useful. But, it helped me form my views and identify any changes.'

'And, was there?' enquired Nick.

'Yes, either signifying the change between our intitially getting an order and retaining it or the change over time reflecting an increasingly competitive environment. The reason I did it this way was to help me get into a different way of thinking about our customers and markets. After a while I found this backward glance unnecessary. And what you have in front of you, as you will see, is an assessment of the relevant order-winners and qualifiers for to-day and in the future.

'Let me explain how I went about it. Mouldings are ordered to the specification of individual customers according to their own requirements. I've identified the order-winners and qualifiers which relate to our customers' current and future needs; that's what the top line shows. And, as you would expect, different order-winners relate to different products. Then I scored each order-winner out of a grand total of 100 points with the total weighting for each adding up to 100. Relevant qualifiers are shown using a capital 'Q'. With me so far?'

'How did you arrive at the weighting for each factor?' Moretti asked.

'By going over current orders, feedback form sales reps, and my own knowledge of the customers and products. Trust me, it's a lot more accurate than calling the clients and asking them. They tend to say what they think you want to hear, or they air their latest gripe. But more importantly they don't seem to know or, if they do, they understandably don't distinguish between the relative importance of the various potential factors. So, this is as accurate as it gets for the time being. The main purpose here is to test the waters. Then we can identify the analysis we will need to undertake in order to verify these initial views.'

'Yes, we'll get to that later,' said Hart. 'Go on, Shirley.'

'Well, I then took the orders and re-arranged them. Instead of grouping by market segment such as food, I grouped by production run or order quantity size. First, you'll notice that this changes the original groupings. There is some consistency, but, there are also some noticeable inconsistencies. Now, notice the differences here. Notice the weightings in the low-volume category. At the very bottom you see that the determining factors are almost all non-manufacturing related. They are things like after-sales service and our own sales ability. Price is invariably a qualifier; delivery speed is an occasional order-winner. There is also quite a high weight attached to the factor that we already supply this customer. You see quality conformance here, and here, but those aren't high weightings and, in fact, are often qualifiers. Basically, we get these low-volume orders because we have sharp salesmen who spot opportunities and because the customers aren't willing to devote the effort it takes to shop around.

'As the orders get slightly bigger, you see delivery speed

creep in more frequently. These factors get more important as the order sizes get larger. And finally you see price starting to matter more. But the bulk of these low-volume orders are not won on manufacturing-related factors.'

'Shirley, just to clarify. These weightings are your initial views based on the analysis you described?' interjected Tony.

'Yes. As we agreed, they are intended as a straw man. We can debate them and change them but, most importantly, the aim is to agree the analyses we need to undertake to verify our different views. Okay so far?

'As we move into the medium-volume category, you see the growing importance of price. Here it scores between 30 and 50 on most products, but there are still other factors; delivery speed and quality conformance are still important. But as the orders get larger, price becomes steadily more important. When you move into high volume, price is usually weighted more heavily and in very high volume it typically scores still higher.

Moretti was frowning at the chart. 'I wish I had seen this earlier. I would have liked to have double-checked the choice of customers and representative orders.'

'I did double-check, in a way. I took the list of representative customers which Tony drew up in advance of our last board meeting and cross-referenced that with the customers from your sample order list. There was variation, but not as much as I expected. I believe we're on broadly the right track. In any case, Nick, we can always increase the sample size when we go on to more detailed analysis later, particularly if there's any doubt. What this chart shows is that differences apparently exist, and it serves as a guide to the things we need to check and verify in order to understand our markets. As you can see, however, segments as we currently describe them do not comprise coherent wholes in terms of the factors which win us orders. Grouping orders based on an order-winner/volume basis cuts across different marketing segments.'

'Why did you pick next year and three years out as your

forward look?'

'I talked this over with several colleagues and we concluded that taking next year and then looking three years on gave the chance to reflect forward. However, it too needs to be discussed and agreed.'

She picked up another chart, nearly identical to the first, and laid it on the table. 'This is the same chart done for the same orders, only using next year's data. Across the board you can see several changes. Some show trends toward one or another order-winner. Increasing order size linked to price, and delivery speed becoming more important as customers are expected to move to just-in-time arrangements. Meanwhile, there are several instances where the role of delivery reliability and quality conformance as qualifers has firmed, signalling the order-losing nature of their provision.

'On the other hand, you can see that some orders have changed in terms of their relevant order-winners and weightings. The consequence is that they are no longer con-sistent with their original segment.

'Now looking three years on you will see similar trends again,' concluded Shirley as she replaced one chart with the other. 'In the medium and high volume segments you can see that our ability to cope with demand increases has, in three or four instances, become a significant factor in winning orders and, in fact, in these two instances we believe it will lead to gaining more market share.

'But also in these segments some products have started to move toward the characteristics of low volume orders. It is expected that order-size will continue to reduce and it is anticipated that the relevant order-winners and qualifers will change accordingly.'

'I suspect that's right,' said Leclerc.

'So do I,' said Hart. 'Now, what have you got to show us on contributions?'

'I've done two things. First, I've taken this same sample of orders, as you can see on this chart, and calculated as a weighted average, order size, actual costs per order, actual contribution per order, contribution as a percentage of sales price and actual contribution per machine hour. Several factors emerge here, some of which seem to contradict each other, and I'm hoping Nick can shed some light on this. Our low-volume products, those with the lowest totals of machine hours and lowest overall contributions, usually make much higher contributions per machine hour. So they earn us less contribution in total because they are smaller orders, but they earn us more contribution per hour; quite considerably more in some cases, although you will see there are one or two noticeable exceptions. Nick, did the figures you gave me include set-up times?'

'No,' said Moretti. 'The machine hour data I gave you only includes run time, when they are actually producing.'

'Right,' said Easton. 'I think we'll have to come back to that as well. This fourth chart compares the results of the third chart with the previous two, which grouped products by volume. There are some correlations of interest. The low-volume orders where non-manufacturing factors are typically the order-winners are the ones which give us the lowest total contributions, but the highest contribution per machine hour. The high and very high volume orders, which are often price sensitive, give low contributions per machine hour, but high total contributions. Again, there are some anomalies which might be worth discussing.

'Look at these two products again. Although very high volume they generate very low contributions per machine hour. Much lower than products for other customers. At the other extreme there is this high-volume order which shows a much higher contribution per hour than all the others with the same level of volume. Then there are these medium-volume orders which begin to look to me like a problem. And finally, at the low-volume end, we have some orders which make low contributions per machine hour.'

There was a short silence. Easton said carefully, 'When I

made that remark about two different businesses, Nick, I was referring to the different patterns associated with low volume and high volume. I'd not seen the machine-hour figures, and I wasn't expecting them to reinforce the image of difference. I don't think for a moment that you really are running two different businesses.'

'No.' Moretti rubbed his chin. 'But it looks from this like I'm running one business in two different directions.'

'What about it?' Hart asked. 'Put this together with what we discussed a few weeks back, about markets and strategy. What does it tell us?'

This time there was a longer silence while Moretti stared fixedly at the four charts. 'It tells me,' he said finally, 'that this is right. It tells me too that we should concentrate in some way on one end of the spectrum or the other. One thing your figures don't tell you, Shirley, is that a single machine is often moving from one product to another, from one volume level to another, all the time. Machine #6, for example, is working on one of your low-volume products right now. We've got a four-cavity mould on it, and it took us four hours to set up; the length of the run is only 12 hours. We'll take that off, put another four-cavity mould on for another product and run it for probably 60 hours. But as with all machines, it is limited in terms of the mould size that will fit. So, if we could put a 16- or 32-cavity mould on that machine, we could cut the running time way back, but we can't. Machine #6 isn't big enough to run big moulds. However, the mix of demand and the mix of machines often does not match.'

'Then that leads to inefficiency,' said Hart. 'Unavoidable, perhaps, but inefficient.'

'It needn't be. At the moment we have a mix of machines handling a mix of customer demands and volumes. We match machines to products and order sizes in order to get the best result in terms of machine utilisation and efficiency. However, if we concentrate on high-volume orders, we could switch to bigger machines and increase volume, thus pumping up our output and profits. Or, we could concentrate on low-volume orders. That would mean smaller machines but more of them, to best cope with the large number of low-volume orders we would take on. Either way, we should increase overall volume and profits.'

He looked up. 'But that's not really a strategy, is it?'

No,' Hart said slowly. 'It isn't a strategy. But it highlights some of the issues we need to address as another step toward developing a strategy. One thing is becoming very clear, strategy is a long haul.'

Chapter 11

"We're no longer working in the dark"

Being a Wednesday, the little restaurant was quiet, and Hart and Wendy were sitting alone at a corner table. Jazz was playing softly on the sound system, and the lights were low. The waiter, who knew the Harts as regulars, brought two glasses of wine and slipped away.

Wendy raised her glass. 'Cheers. How did your day go?'

'Quite well, for a change. I've got some charts I'd like to show you later; I'd like your opinion.' He checked. 'Sorry. I swore to myself I wasn't going to talk about work tonight.'

She was watching him rather carefully. She was wearing a black dress which Hart thought made her look extremely attractive, and he was hoping to hold onto that thought. But she said, 'Why not? I don't mind in the least.'

'Don't you? It's not something we discuss much these days.'

'Don't we? I hadn't noticed.'

He was not sure how to reply to that. He studied the menu for a moment, even though he knew it by heart, and finally she said, 'How is your strategy exercise coming on?'

'It's . . . getting there. We made a bit of progress today, I think. We almost had a civil war on our hands after Shirley made a joke to Nick about splitting the business in half. Poor old Nick doesn't think things like that are very funny.'

'Maybe it wasn't a joke,' Wendy said speculatively. 'It's what I'm thinking of doing.'

'What?' All his resolve about not talking about business flew out the window; they were talking about it, almost naturally. 'Are you really?'

'Really truly.' She smiled slightly. 'You may not believe it, but what you said to me several weeks ago actually did sink in. I began to wonder what I was doing, running a top-flight gallery, a restoration business, a chain of print shops, and prospectively, an *objets d'art* outlet in the tourist market all out of one office in Toronto and using the same rules and criteria. My staff and I were being pulled in every direction at once, and it was hard on our nerves and hard on morale. I've been working like a slave, but I think I've solved the problem.'

'What are you doing?'

'Like I said, I'm splitting the business up into units. It's risky, but I think all the different business activities are big enough now to handle it. They are certainly all different enough from one another to make it seem worthwhile. The way I'm thinking now, each unit will to have its own manager, its own accounts, its own marketing plan, everything separate. Chope Galleries and the restoration business stay together as I think they belong together. They attract the same sorts of people, albeit with different wants, and there's a lot of crossover. The gallery manager will take over responsibility for both. The print and frame shops go into a second division, with a single manager overseeing the lot and taking the load of day-to-day operations away from me. The *objets d'art* become a third division, managed directly by me for the time being, but ultimately coming under their own manager as well. That leaves me on my own at the top.'

'This third division,' he said. 'That's if you go into Ottawa.'

'I am going into Ottawa, John. I haven't got a site yet, but as soon as I do, we're setting up shop.' She leaned forward. 'Don't you see? This organisation gives me the flexibility to do that. I can go on from Ottawa and expand these shops into a second chain, put another outlet in downtown Toronto, one in Kingston maybe, and certainly one in Montreal. This is my way forward. This is what I want to do.'

'So you'll have three different divisions all working in different directions. Who is going to control them all?'

'Well, that's my role,' said Wendy, obviously excited and pleased with herself, 'I'll be at the top.' She continued with a smile, 'I'll issue orders and minions will rush to obey. I shall provide direction and delegate the action to others. And, a key part in that control is to think through the performance measures which relate to each business. Once I realised the key role that this dimension had in this decision, I was home and dry. To-date, I've looked at the whole business in the same way while intuitively recognising difference but not overtly

145

separating it out. That led to confusion and added to the complexity. Now I see the businesses as they are, different to one another, competing with different order-winners and qualifiers, if I may borrow a phrase,' she said with a smile. 'And, my role at the top will be based on testing and evaluating decisions and proposals against the strategy for each business. If it fits I know it will enhance the business. If it doesn't then I'll be inclined to say "no".'

'But, what about developments leading to improved efficiency,' queried John.

'You're right. I would separate investments leading to efficiency from those concerned with enhancing effectiveness. The former would be stand alone decisions based on their own merits.'

There was a short silence before an excited Wendy continued. 'I can do it now, John. I've such good people working for me, they really are the best. Janine Lee, this new girl I hired last year to run the gallery, you've met her? She's dynamite, and she's absolutely dying to be let off the leash and show what she can do. Of course I'll watch what they all do, very carefully, to make sure they don't stray off course. But I can do that and still think about what I want to do next and where I want to go next.'

'My God,' he said quietly. 'You really do have it all figured out, don't you?'

'No, of course not. There's a lot of hard work ahead, but I know I can do it. . . . John, I thought you'd be happy about this.'

'You know my feelings. You know I think this is the wrong move, and you're diversifying too far. And as far as splitting the business goes, what about the potential loss of control? What about economies of scale? If you duplicate all your finance and accounting functions, it will cost you more. And presumably each business unit would do its own hiring and its own advertising? More duplication. . . . The waiter is coming back, I think we'd better order.'

They ordered, quietly, and then waited a few moments after the waiter had gone. Hart said, 'I'm sorry. It's not my business, and you know what is right better than me. I suppose I feel resentful at you for being so positive and seeing your way ahead so clearly, whether you're right about it or not. I'm not so lucky. I said to you we made some progress today, but I don't really think it was very much.'

'You're overly critical,' said Wendy, 'of yourself, of your company and of me.'

She was obviously smarting, and the perfunctory apology hadn't made much difference. 'I know it,' he said quietly. 'The truth is, things aren't turning out as I thought they would. I feel like I've been too cautious all along, and I would like to do something really radical. I would like to start over from scratch.'

'It can't be done,' said Wendy, calming down a little. 'You've got to take where you are as a starting point and get on. And then, by all means, do something radical. Maybe your Shirley Easton was onto something.'

'Maybe. I'll run it by Ian when I talk to him. I'm about ready to try anything. The problem with Macallister is he tends to lay out the options for you and then sit back with a bland look on his face and tell you the choice is yours.'

'Well, it is.'

'I know it is! But at this time I'm looking for guidance. I was never trained for this, either at business school or in my working career. And if I, the CEO, hasn't been trained for it, then everyone else will find it difficult to cope. I need an expert's point of view.'

'He's giving you an expert's point of view. Trust him. You're not being very fair, you know, think of the help he has given you so far. He's the one who got you started thinking about this at all. He's providing you with stimulus for thought and an independent, outside point of view of what is happening in your business. That's vitally important in it's own right.'

'Is it? You don't place much weight on my point of view.'

147

'I place a great deal of weight on your point of view, and I always consider what you say. But I reserve the right to think you may be wrong. In the end, it is my business and my decision. Ian will tell you the same thing, as indeed he probably has.'

He smiled, a little bitterly. 'And what's he been telling you about your business?'

'What makes you think he's been telling me anything?' Wendy asked.

On Thursday morning, after a troubled night's sleep, Hart called Macallister. 'How are you, Ian? I want to call another review meeting, next week if we can manage it, and I'd like you there. I want to fax you some charts and other data which our analysis program has generated. Can you take a look at these and then make some recommendations?'

'Sure.' Macallister as ever sounded positive and confident. 'So you think the moment has come, do you?'

'I think we're as close as we're ever going to get, and I also don't think we can wait any longer. Time spent now is time wasted. We've got to make some decisions.'

'Fair enough. Fix a time for your meeting, and then let my secretary know. I'll make sure I'm free. Now, what exactly are you sending me?'

Hart looked down at Shirley Easton's charts, which were lying on his desk. 'We've taken a new sample of orders and have generated all the information on contributions and machine times that you suggested. We have some separate information on materials cost that you also suggested, but we haven't broken it down by order.'

'I'll do that myself. Have you got cost figures for set-up times?'

'We do, but again, those are separate. As you know, we don't build those into machine times.'

'Fine. One other thing. For each of the orders you're sending me, can someone look up and note the lead time for each order and add that to the data? Whether the customer wanted the order in five days, 20 days or whatever. I assume you'll have that information on your original order sheets.'

'Yes. All right, I'll get someone onto that. It might take a day or so, so I'll send you the rest of the data straight away.'

The charts were faxed that afternoon and returned with alacrity. Across the control sheet Ian had scribbled, 'These look great. My congratulations to whoever did all this. Sample may not be perfect, but it's good enough for present purposes. Two queries: One, you've listed all these factors as being potential order-winners; have you thought about which qualifiers could be order-losing sensitive? And two, you've figured out contributions per machine-hour and overall per product. Now compare actual to estimated contributions per hour and also actual contribution to the weighting given to price as an order-winner. Finally, include set-up times as part of the overall machine time for each order, and then do the calculation again, like I did at the last meeting. If you can't get them exact, get as close as you can.'

Hart showed this to Shirley Easton the following morning. She said, 'I wonder what he means by "order-losing sensitive"? In my view you either win an order or you don't.'

Hart said, 'I think Ian is asking us to identify any qualifiers that, if we fail to provide, may quickly result in losing an order. Certainly we have lost orders through failure to meet customer needs on more than one occasion very possibly because we didn't correctly read the importance the customer attached to a qualifier. What about the other points?'

'I think I can guess where those links are leading. I'll run an analysis as soon as I can and tell you what comes out. I'll prepare a new analysis with the set-up times as well.'

She found him at lunchtime in the staff canteen, sitting down to a turkey sandwich and a cup of coffee. 'Well, well, surprise, surprise,' she said. 'There's often a noticeable discrepancy between actual and estimated contributions per hour and, in some instances, a marked difference between levels of actual contribution and our view of price as an order-winner. Also, including set-up times as part of total machine hours changes the outcomes and, in some instances, it is a marked change. It certainly gives us more insights into where we are making money and also dispels some of our perceptions in terms of attractive and less attractive business. It makes an interesting new way of slicing it, doesn't it? Nick will be most interested when I show him.'

'It certainly is starting to afford new insight into our orders, the way we use existing capacity, profit margins and the potential impact on the business of alternative directions.'

'Which is what we've been needing to know all along, certainly with regard to Laurentian's questions about where we wanted to go as a company and their request for a strategic justification to increase production.'

'Which is why we're doing all this in the first place.' Hart said. 'We're no longer working in the dark. We're beginning to know what we are, what we want and why we want it. Doesn't that make you feel better?'

'Can I get back to you on that?' asked Easton.

Ian Macallister arrived by taxi 20 minutes before the meeting, on an afternoon when the temperature had dropped and low clouds were threatening to usher in an early evening. In Hart's office he dropped his coat and briefcase on one chair and sat down in another. 'God, I'm tired. It's one thing after another at the moment. I've just taken on a new client in Ottawa, a paper company which is riddled with inefficiencies; it's overmanned, its machines are out of date, there are severe quality problems. They've got double figure reject rates on some projects, and yet they can't quite seem to figure out what's wrong. They know there's a problem, but they're convinced it's mostly, if not all, the fault of their customers.'

'Sounds a bit like us,' said Hart.

'John, in relative terms you guys are easy to work with. A straightforward problem with a solution bound to emerge somewhere down the road, and best of all, I know you're actually trying.'

Hart sat down behind his desk. 'Well, that's nice to hear. I'm particularly relieved to hear that someone has faith in us. So what is this afternoon's agenda?'

'Today, we're going to talk through strategy. I think you're ready for it. Six weeks ago you'd probably not have been receptive to the concepts and ideas we're going to talk about. Now, perhaps, you'll listen, and nod, and say to yourselves, "Hey, maybe some of this stuff is relevant to us after all." I forgot to mention, is there an overhead projector ready in the boardroom?'

'I'll have one brought up.'

'Good. I can't function properly without an overhead projector. I sometimes think I need one in order to breathe.' Macallister took a gulp of his coffee, characteristically forgetting to check how hot it was and burned his tongue. Hart watched him in amusement. It suddenly dawned on him that Macallister was showing signs of nerves. So far, all he had had to do was make suggestions about what Wentworth ought to be doing. Now, he had to lay his own beliefs and philosophies on the line, and there was always a chance that the assembled directors and managers would reject them. Whether you were right or wrong became immaterial when there was pride, emotion and subjectivity involved.

He picked up the phone and asked Darlene to arrange for the overhead projector and then the two of them sat in silence for a few minutes, finishing their coffee. 'Ready?' Hart asked.

'Sure.' Macallister picked up his briefcase and followed Hart along the corridor.

Once everyone was present Hart said simply, 'Right, let's make a start. First, Ian is going to make a short presentation and comment on the analysis we have done so far. Then we'll have questions and general discussion. If you're ready, Ian.'

Macallister stood up and walked to the overhead projector, carrying a file folder full of acetates in one hand. If he had been nervous, he didn't show it now; he looked relaxed and confident, and watching him it was hard not to feel optimistic. So much of this is psychological, Hart thought; knowing you can find a solution, knowing that it can be simple and that goals can be achieved is half the battle. Or at least, I hope it is.

'Let's go back to our earlier meeting,' suggested Macallister, 'and reflect on what strategies are and how they work. This will probably sound a little like a lecture, but please bear with me. Corporate strategy is the output of functions like manufacturing and marketing debating and agreeing in which markets they wish to compete.

'Having a future as well as a current dimension, firms are often hidebound by their past investments and commercial histories. Even so, knowing the markets they are in and what tasks that sets for the various functions is a core strategic issue facing all companies. The need for functional debate is fundamental to strategy developments and consequent outputs. Only by understanding the essential perspectives of the different functions in the business can companies address the implications for being successful in their chosen markets.

'For most companies, this is far from how strategy is developed. More typically executives are charged with developing a strategy for their own function, and they do so independently of other functions. Corporate strategy documents, therefore, are usually in large binders and inside are sections containing these separate functional strategies. The nearest these functional strategies get to being interrelated one to another is when they sit side by side in this same binder.' Macallister was clearly hitting his stride.

'In place of strategies based on interfunctional debate and an essential understanding of key perspectives, many companies put forward strategic statements, the purpose of which is to be all-inclusive. The outcomes are general, all-embracing statements devoid of the clarity and insights essential to strategy.

Think of the insights you all have gained since we started this project.

'Strategy is a distillation process. Its aim is to identify the essence of the business in terms of its current and future markets, the order-winners and qualifiers which relate to those markets and to establish functional strategies which support these. The strategies should prioritise the investments and developments within a function, while the choice of markets, as I stressed earlier, is the outcome of functional debate. Strategic direction is thus agreed to with an understanding of the functional investments and timescales involved. In this way, a company can develop a strategic prioritising mechanism, and build relevant support for its chosen market.'

'So,' interjected Shirley, 'all the stuff Nick and I have been sparring over is really just functional debate?'

Everyone welcomed the chance to laugh. Macallister smiled, joining in the moment, before continuing.

'Manufacturing's strategic contribution is being able to support a company's markets better than the manufacturing functions of competitors. To do this the company needs to make appropriate investments in both processes (machines) and the infrastructure (support staff and functions). The overriding problem, however, is that manufacturing investments are both large and fixed. They cost a lot and take a long time to secure and implement and even a longer time to change. So, it's essential that companies know what they're buying.'

'So, where do most companies start?' asked Hart.

Macallister took a sip of coffee and continued. 'Unfortunately, most companies start their strategic debate with a statement of corporate objectives such as growth and measures of financial performance. Yours, for instance, are to increase profit, with overall sales growth as a secondary goal probably contingent on the first. Companies then turn to marketing, as you have done, and ask for its strategy to achieve these. Marketing then puts forward its views covering markets, products and sales forecasts. This part of the corporate debate tends to happen in most companies as it is essential to the business planning procedure. However, that step is typically where the strategy debate ends. The rest is thought to be linear and deterministic. The assumption which follows is that the other functions, including manufacturing, can meet these strategies. The problem is, therefore, how does a function like manufacturing get into the strategy debate at the right time and the right level? My answer is to force a debate about a company's markets as these debates are the linking mechanism between functions at the strategy level.'

'Hence the in-depth debate we are undertaking. But tell me,' continued Moretti, 'how does what we currently do fit into the current way of developing a business?'

Macallister nodded. 'If companies typically restrict market debate to the perspective of marketing in the way I described, there is no mechanism for linking functions into market needs. Marketing perspectives don't yield these. Without strategic context other functions react to the demands placed on them as best they can. This leads to functions seeing their role as one of supporting whatever is required. In addition, this has also, I believe, led to investing in panacea-type solutions under the guise of strategy.

'Don't get one wrong. All functions have a management and control aspect to the executive task as well as a responsibility to discharge those tasks as efficiently as possible. Thus initiatives directed to improving these elements of what they do are both necessary and essential. However, there is also a strategic element to the task and this has to be fashioned around the needs of a company's markets. Without this, functions will endeavour to take appropriate developments and investments in terms of what they think the business requires and not on the basis of agreed market needs.

'This is why,' continued Macallister, 'I suggested you look at your markets, review them by collecting data and so help you re-assess them. Marketing's view of markets identifies segments based on that function's perspective. For example as here, by industrial sector. However, these reviews do not identify the demands customers make in terms of order-winners and qualifiers. Nor are they intended to. But, without these additional insights, the assumption made is that the similarity inherent in, say, sector type can be translated into other dimensions. The issue facing you is to develop functional support for your markets. For marketing's perspective, industrial sector is a key split. But, this will not be so for manufacturing. Linking manufacturing to your markets needs to be based on the different sets of tasks required.

'What companies find is what you are finding. Invariably there will be differences within a segment in terms of what the various customers within a segment demand. The order winners and qualifiers are not consistent between segments. Often too this difference extends to customers within a segment. To decide on a course of action, you need to have these insights. Without them, you will assume that growing sales in one segment and reducing your selling effort in another segment will be a sound strategy. Already from the initial data here, this is manifestly not so. And, this is not surprising.'

Macallister paused and then placed a transparency onto the overhead projector.

'The following diagrams represent the issues we have been discussing. Most companies set objectives and then link marketing strategy to these as the way of assessing their

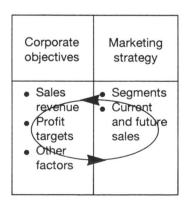

viability. I know that you do this as part of your corporate planning procedure.

These sales forecasts are used to assess factors such as profit projections and future capacity requirements. As the circle shows, these steps and their consequences are debated. In fact, it has been known in companies for CEOs to ask marketing for a re-think on sales forecasts as the first attempt doesn't yield the desired objectives. But, I assume not here.' Macallister stopped. Suddenly everyone realised the humour of their own reality and smiled.

Macallister too allowed a brief smile before continuing. 'The critical issue is that this is where the strategy debate ends. The assumption is that relevant functions can deliver on these requirements. Traditionally this has led to functions developing strategies which are independent of one another and the market place.

'So, how can, say, manufacturing get into the strategic debate at the right time and at the right level. This link, as I emphasised earlier, is by answering the question "How do you win orders in your various markets?" This transparency,' Macallister continued as he replaced one with another, 'shows the link.'

Corporate objectives	Marketing strategy	How do you win orders in the market place?	Manufacturing strategy	
			process choice	infrastructure

• Sales revenue
• Profit targets
• Other factors
	• Segments
	• Current and future sales
		• Price
		• Quality conformance
		• Delivery
		  – speed
		  – reliability
		• Brand name
			• Alternatives
			• Trade-offs
			• Capacity
			• Role of inventory
				• Systems procedures
				• Functional support

'The arrow from left to right represents the fact that the centre segment is a restatement of a company's markets. The arrow from right to left reflects the fact that the market prioritises manufacturing's strategic developments and investments. And let me again reinforce the point that although the framework implies a set of steps, this is not so. I've represented it this way to facilitate explanation.

'The reality of strategy debate is a process inviting statement and re-statement built around the exchange of perspectives and the introduction of data and new insights. As I mentioned earlier, steps one and two are typically undertaken in an interactive way, with feedback loops, each influencing the other. Steps four and five are usually thought to be linear and deterministic. There is little, if any, cross-linking.

'Using the traditional approach means that manufacturing, by definition, is only there to support the decisions marketing has made, and that cannot be a logical course of action.'

'It's wrong from a logical point of view,' observed Hart, 'because what a company like ours actually does is make and sell products. What we sell is not our marketing effort alone; the essential support we provide to customers and the meeting of their needs comes from several different functions. And, all these functions need to have their own perspective taken into account.

'That's right,' said Macallister. 'Such functional myopia is rarely sound from the overall view of a business. By applying a marketing focus exclusively companies force their production systems to do things they were never designed to do, and that mistake will adversely affect the bottom line. Most manufacturing companies today treat their manufacturing systems by coaxing them, bullying and/or chasing them if they are out of line. And that is typically done without adequate understanding of what their capabilities are.

'Don't misunderstand me, Nick. Once upon a time our companies were ruled by the production men, and they treated marketing as a Cinderella function. That similarly was a mistake. Well, letting marketing take over responsibility for the direction of the company doesn't make sense either. The answer is to have all parts of the company – marketing, design, production, finance and personnel – working in harmony.'

'That's a great idea, you say. The question is how do you get there? How do you do that when as you have begun to see from your own analysis, markets are fragmented, diverse and ever-changing? How does a static manufacturing base cope with the dynamics of your markets? How can you expect marketing to sell into dozens of market segments, meeting the needs of hundreds of individual customers, thousands of different products and potential products, and then hand them all over together with their wide-ranging sets of technical and business specifications to one set of fixed capabilities called "manu-facturing" and expect any kind of harmony to result?'

Macallister looked around the table. Nick Moretti was sitting bolt upright in his chair, staring fixedly at the overhead projector screen. Hart thought, he's guessed what's coming. Hart himself had guessed some time before; his mind was still circling round the idea, trying to get used to it.

'You don't,' said Macallister. 'You get instead what we have in most companies today; a manufacturing strategy which is not set by the manufacturing division, a marketing strategy which operates on a completely different plane and only connects with the manufacturing side in order to issue orders. You also get a production operation which is increasingly being left behind by the dynamics of the markets it is supposed to be serving. What about it? Have I described the case correctly?'

'Speaking as someone who is in neither marketing nor manu-facturing,' said Tim Pringle, 'I'd say you hit the nail pretty well on the head. I can add another factor. We're in pay negotiations with our staff at the moment, and I would say 90 percent of them have no idea what they are producing, why they are producing it or what the priorities are. It's not just a question of organising the system, but of motivating the people who run it.'

Macallister nodded. 'But there is a way to avoid all this,' he said. 'It's quite a simple way, and it involves quite a simple psychological step. In your own minds, you need to restore manufacturing, not to a dominant role, but to an *equal* position with all the other parts of the company. While you're analysing your markets, you need also to be analysing your manufacturing processes and infrastructure. And the decisions you make about markets must be made in line with existing and future decisions on these two facets of manufacturing.'

Macallister reached across and switched off the overhead projector. Then he added, 'Strategy needs to be based on the bigger picture. That goal requires debate, an interchange based on understanding and agreement on current and future markets. This debate is long, hard and on-going. Remember, the most significant orders are the ones to which you say "no", for these mark the boundaries and indicate which markets you are not in. You've got to lay out these boundaries and stick to them. And, any changes to these come through the same level of understanding and debate.

'The key issue in strategy, therefore, concerns an understanding of the relevant issues and perspectives of functions as linked to the current and future markets in which you decide you wish to compete.

'Now, let's put this into context with Wentworth. I have seen your analysis to date, and I would agree that it is beginning to reflect some key differences. The numbers may need verifying, and you will need to complete the same analysis on a larger representative sample. It is from this that you will draw a more complete picture. You've highlighted some of the problems you face and some of the choices you have to make. No, that's not quite true. You've looked at some of the choices you have to make. But you haven't looked at all of them, and you haven't yet got a true perspective on your own organisation.

'The data and analysis I received was excellent, as far as it went. But look at how you are figuring your costs.' The overhead projector went back on, and Macallister put another transparency on the screen. 'Here is your own assessment of costs for the sample orders. And here is mine, including set-up times. The picture, as we noticed before, reveals important differences. But, we also need data that relate to other relevant order-winners and qualifiers.

'To start with, I asked for data on delivery lead times. Well, I added this information as part of a further review of customers and their orders. As you will see from this,' continued Macallister as he slipped another transparency onto the projector, 'some customers consistently require shorter lead times than others. As you know, this puts more pressure on manufacturing and other systems. This not only incurs cost, but also affects the business's ability to respond to the needs of other customers. You will see from these two customers that the contribution per hour, including set ups, is below average for the sample, but they also require short lead times. On the other hand this customer requires short lead times, but the orders give very high contributions per hour, while these three customers give average or somewhat below average contributions, but give long lead times. As you can begin to see, without these insights it is impossible to know which markets and which customers within which markets you should go for. If this small sample is truly representative, and, as I stressed earlier you must broaden the sample base as these insights are critical to your decisions, then not all food and cosmetic customers are good and the reverse holds elsewhere.

'Now you have begun to identify market differences and also to show that not all customers in a particular segment are the same. To grow this business profitably, which, if I may remind you, is your objective, then selecting not only segments, but customers within a segment, is key. And the basis for making that choice is, in part, the data you collect on what actually happens. Phasing out, stimulating growth, proactively working in key dimensions then becomes a joint decision by the business as a whole.'

'What happens,' interjected Leclerc, 'if we in marketing argue it is essential to keep a below-average contribution customer because of potential future business.'

'Two things,' responded Macallister. 'The first is to recognise that this is a business not a functional decision.'

'Could you explain that?' Pringle asked.

'Sure. I'm simply stressing the need for companies to recognise that decisions like these need to be shared and agreed by the business as a whole. Only in that way can coordinated understanding and response be ensured. In the same way functions partake in co-ordinated strategies which include identifying their role in securing overall success. This leads me to my next point which is that you would need to collect data on the size of the "underperformance" over time and check whether or not the potential growth actually took place. What is more, I would also recommend you consider calculating the profit impact of this type of decision and recording it as a marketing charge. This is not to shift the blame, but is a recognition of the fact that these "costs" are part of marketing's decisions. To me, they are the same as advertising – a way to boost future sales.

'But, if I may,' suggested Macallister, 'let me return to the main line of my argument. The procedure you are following is to better understand how you can meet your corporate objectives. At the moment, although sales are growing, profits are not, and this within the context of a lack of additional capacity. Also, your past investment decisions have provided a mix of trade-offs which are in conflict, apparently, with the proposed marketing strategy.'

Shirley jumped in now. 'The data we are collecting is simply to help us move away from the broad brush approach needed to develop strategy to one where we have a greater understanding of our markets. Right, Ian?'

'Yes, without this you are in the dark. You will be making key strategic decisions without adequate understanding. As you have seen already, strategic arguments to grow the food and cosmetic sectors of your business and reduce your efforts in other segments would have been based on the assumption that each segment is a consistent whole. This is clearly not so. You will need to question these decisions in the light of what you now know. Similarly, data on the other order-winners and qualifiers will give you further essential insights.

'When all this is completed, you will be faced with a number of strategic decisions which will encompass both the dimensions of marketing and manufacturing. And, you will need to reconcile these in terms of what's best overall for your business.

'To-date, you have begun to consider specialising. On the table, as I understand it, you see the choice as between specialising in high-volume, low-margin products or in low-volume products where the factors of delivery speed and quality are more important than price. We need to debate that choice extensively, but I am also aware that time is getting short, and I'm going to have to hurry things along. I'm going to ask you to identify the key process and infrastructure requirements necessary to support these markets. Can you do that?'

The silence lasted for perhaps 15 seconds. Well, Ian my lad, Hart reflected, you haven't been my favourite person in the world for the last couple of weeks, especially because your name keeps appearing on my wife's lips, but I've got to hand it to you. You've provided all of us with key insights into the business, challenged our basic views about our functions and past approaches and given us a way to connect these previously disparate parts within the context of what's best for Wentworth. You've got all my managers fired up and ready to run. They're ready to go.

They were ready, and they were looking at him. They wanted a lead. As CEO, it was up to him to give them one.

He cleared his throat. 'Thank you. That was, if I may say so, well articulated. A lecture, an explanation and a challenge all in one. Well, everyone, I think Ian has added greater clarity to our discussions, more than we could have made ourselves. Who wants to kick off?'

Tony Leclerc leaned forward. 'I'm listening to all this with a very odd sensation because, of course, I'm clearing out and leaving Wentworth in six weeks. So, in a sense, none of this will affect me directly. On the other hand, I'm going to face exactly the same set of problems in my next job, so I guess I have more than a vested interest in seeing what the solution is going to look like. Ian, I understand, or I think I understand. As you said yourself, manufacturing is inherently fixed while markets are inherently dynamic. How can we make them match, you ask? Well, isn't it an impossible task? Should we even try? Why not just get on with what we've got? Marketing-led businesses can and do work very well, and Wentworth has in the past been a very successful company. Why not stick with that and look to marketing to find solutions?'

'How many of you,' said Macallister, 'are familiar with Greek mythology? How many of you know the story of the Gordian Knot? It was promised that the man who could untie it would rule the world. Many tried, but none could ever work out its intricacies. All failed, until Alexander the Great came along. He didn't even try to untie the knot. He cut it in two with his sword, and the prophecy came true.

'This is a Gordian Knot. You don't try to unravel the intricacies of making fixed manufacturing capabilities and dynamic markets match. You don't puzzle out this problem. You *cut* it. You choose a solution that recognises market differences and matches them with appropriate manufacturing capabilities.'

'And what sort of solution,' said Tim Pringle, 'would fit our problem?'

'I can suggest one possibility which has worked in other companies. Your markets are fragmented and diverse; you can do nothing about that, except cut out the ones that don't make you adequate profits and work harder in the ones that do. But you can focus your manufacturing processes and, in turn, your infrastructure, on the various and even diverse markets you want to be in.'

'But don't you have to choose a market on which to focus? You can't focus the plant in two different directions, can you?'

'Well, why not?' said Macallister. 'If you have two or more different and profitable markets, why not support them both? Divide the plant. Divide the infrastructure. Split manufacturing and other parts of the company into different focused units, each oriented to a given market, and line up the processes and infrastructure to the individual needs of each chosen market. You're going to have to cut the knot. Otherwise, you'll continue trying unsuccessfully to undo the complexity you, and most businesses, have to face.'

Chapter 12

"Easing our way into the process"

'But you can't do that!' said Nick Moretti incredulously. Shirley Easton, who had unfortunately chosen to sit beside him, was looking studiously at her nails.

'You can't just split the plant into two or three bits, just like that! And as for breaking up all the infrastructure functions, well why do you think those have been centralised in the first place?'

'Go on,' said Macallister patiently. 'Why have they been centralised in the first place?'

'To concentrate specialists and gain economies of scale! You can't have three production scheduling departments and three tool rooms and three who knows what else, not in a company this size, the costs would be astronomical!'

'I agree,' said Alan Mills, speaking for the first time, 'I think the costs would be, as Nick says, astronomical. And it isn't just duplication of function. I can see that by assigning people to different tasks, we could actually get away with very little duplication. But there are cost control implications. Do you then propose three different purchasing units as well, all on the market buying raw materials in three different lots, all paying separately, all keeping their own records, all running their own finances? Isn't that the very opposite of the greater efficiency we're striving for?'

'Well let me go back a step,' said Macallister. 'First, most companies develop their organisation using the principles of economies of scale and control through specialists. Yours is no exception. For most of us, this is also the only organisational format we know. If you reflect, however, on the markets best suited to these principles, the answer would be those reflecting the characteristics of high volume and stability. However, today most markets are neither high-volume nor stable. Looking at your own, this is clearly so.

'It's not, therefore, that the principles of economies of scale and control through specialists are unsound, it's that their application in today's markets is inappropriate.

'Secondly, the challenge I have made does not imply that

there are only two points on this continuum of organisational structure – on the one hand, current approaches, or, on the other, for plants to split down into smaller units on every dimension of structure.

'Third, and something I can't promise, what normally happens when companies split their manufacturing capability on the basis of the principle of focus is that total overhead decrease costs.'

'To explain why, let me first say a few things about focused plants. Using as their basis the principles of economies of scale and control through specialists, today's businesses meet the needs of their different markets through the same set of facilities. As markets are increasingly different, however, many companies are finding this approach is counter productive. To cope with the increasing levels of complexity, specialists have to-date typically advocated increasingly complex solutions with attendant overhead, but without the cost accounting systems to reflect what accounts for what. The outcome is that a large part of total cost is not adequately reflected in corporate decisions.

'Focus splits a business by aligning parts of both processes and infrastructure to different markets using key order-winners. The outcome is the creation of units required to support a similar set of demands. To do this, processes and infrastructures are allocated to each unit except where it makes more sense (normally in terms of investment) to leave them centralised. So, the rule is to split except where that would result in an unacceptable duplication of investment. Other processes and infrastructures are then split in terms of the needs of each focused unit.

'However, another by-product of current organisational structures is that the need for the large overhead costs is not understood. With focus, the lack of understanding is replaced by a greater awareness. As a result costs decrease as the need and role of existing overhead is challenged.

'However,' concluded Macallister, 'if it doesn't make sense, don't do it.'

There was a pause while they all stared, waiting for him to continue. Hart leaned forward. 'I think what's meant here is not a mandate to split the company up, but rather a mandate to analyse our markets, assess the degree of similarity within them and review our current approach to supporting them. How far we go needs to be bounded by what's best for our business overall. I think what we need is to focus on the key tasks of our business, making and selling products. We have to take on board the fact that manufacturing is at the decision-making end along with marketing. As far as infrastructure and support go, well, we need to examine them in detail and see what makes most sense.

'Frankly, Alan, I can visualise a situation where each focused unit, if that's what we want to call them, has its own scheduling department and may develop and maintain its own costing function. Equally, some centralised functions, such as finance, and some aspects of personnel would tend to remain centralised. And, if we think that such changes will improve our effectiveness as a business, then we ought to move that way.

'The question, of course, is will it lead to overall improvement? That's what we have to decide. What options have we got in creating separate operating units focused on different markets? On what markets ought we to focus? How ought we to focus and to what extent?

'What we need to do is to push the analyses further to better understand our markets. Without this, we can't move forward. However, may I ask you all to start thinking through the issues around focus. It's not that this is what we're going to do, but we do need to get our minds around the issues.

'This is not a marketing problem or a manufacturing problem. It's a company problem, which affects everybody in Wentworth. Think about it and think hard. Our time is running out.'

Back in his office, after the meeting was over, Hart said, 'Thank you, Ian. That was a good session, and I think it's just what we all needed.'

'I put the cat among the canaries, though, didn't I? I'm sorry about that. It's not part of my task to make your job more difficult.'

'My managers are professional enough to be able to cope. I'm more concerned about the fact that I'm going to get five completely different opinions from them, plus my own views, and am going to be faced with the task of reconciling them all. I know it's my job, but I can't say I look forward to it.'

'You'll do well at it,' said Macallister with confidence. 'That little speech of yours at the end was just the right touch. Real leadership stuff. I'm impressed.'

'And surprised? Come on, Ian. You weren't sure I could do it, were you?'

'I was, as it happens,' said Macallister abruptly. He looked at his watch. 'Well, it's been fun, but I think I'd better be getting off. My plane leaves in an hour. Can I use your phone to get a taxi?'

'I'll drive you. It's the least I can do.'

But though they did talk desultorily about timing and future meetings, they travelled most of the journey in silence. Hart felt he did not know what to say, and Macallister, obviously very tired, slumped in his seat, half asleep. Only at the airport did Macallister say, 'From now on, I'll be involved a lot more, if you want me. It's here, where you're planning the shape of reorganisation, that my experience can probably come in handy. When you want some help, 'phone. I can always come down on the weekend again.'

Thanks. I'll keep it in mind.'

'Regards to Wendy.' Macallister walked off through the rain towards the door of the airport terminal, and Hart started the engine and pulled the Bronco out onto the road for the drive home.

He arrived a little after 8:00, and the house was dark. He walked through from the garage flicking on lights and then the answering machine. The only message was from Wendy; she was going to be late, something had come up, and it might be 10:00 before she was home. She would get something to eat in the city, and he didn't need to wait up.

Her voice had the perfectly neutral tone she used when someone else was in the office with her – or when something was wrong. He turned off the machine and went to the bar cabinet; his hand, hovering over the wine bottle, moved suddenly to a seldom opened bottle of whisky. He poured a small drink, added a healthy dose of soda and walked across the living room to stand and stare out the dark window, drink in hand.

The rain had been coming down faster as he drove home, and now it was beating hard against the window. He thought, we have arrived at a crossroads. Or have we? I can remember thinking this before, several times in the past few weeks. Are there going to be more surprises lying in wait? Blast Macallister; why can't the man simply tell us from the start what we have to do, and then help us get on with it.

The answer Hart told himself, is that you don't teach calculus until you have taught basic mathematics, and you don't teach managers (or CEOs) strategy until you have taught them a few basic facts about the nature of markets and manufacturing. We had to ease our way into the process; having someone come along and impose a set of approaches on us from the outside would have been a failure. Most of us would not have known what was going on. Some of us would have resisted, if only in a passive way, and I would have lost the key support of a team of good managers.

Be honest, John Hart. Your current unease about Ian Macallister is due to reasons so illogical and unfounded that you dare not even admit them to yourself. You have no reason to dislike this man, an old friend, or to be impolite to him, as you very nearly were this evening. This is business. Be a professional and concentrate on the real problem at hand. There are decisions which must be made, and soon. If you don't report something back to Laurentian by the end of May, when Tony leaves, they are going to assume that you can't handle the problem.

He stood irresolute. He was torn between training and instinct. All his experience to date told him that there was only one good way to run a manufacturing operation and that was how they were doing it at the moment. You consolidated production and infrastructure as much as you possibly could in order to cut costs and concentrate the level of expertise. You directed your marketing effort toward expanding business on the assumption that more business was good business. You organised your company as a single, linear unit. It made sound, economic sense.

But instinct plus those blasted figures on the page, told him that this system had worked well while the economy in general and the company in particular had been expanding, when markets were high volume and stable. But these principles were not working now when markets were becoming increasingly different and greater volume instability was creeping in. And instinct also told him – was it instinct, or the cold voice of logic, which cared nothing for conventions and 'how things had always been done'. If marketing strategy concerned identifying segments and developing approaches to meet their differences then manufacturing needed to do the same. Except that manufacturing's view of the market would be based on the order-winners and qualifiers that manufacturing had to provide – that Macallister's suggestions were right. Since markets were becoming increasingly different, then a company would need to learn how to cope with difference. If not, then it might as well get out of the business altogether. The outcome, therefore, was that you were going to have to split your manufacturing processes and infrastructure.

That sounded right. Everything about it seemed right at first hearing. But did it make economic sense? He felt faintly amused, for the first time that day, that there seemed to be a

171

divergence between logic and economics. Would the excess costs, which even Macallister admitted would be incurred, but in reality might not show themselves, really justify the improved efficiency and greater focus anticipated?

What would Laurentian say if he proposed a strategic plan whereby the parent company was to provide him with investment so he could increase his manufacturing costs?

All the same, something would have to be done. That was the irritating thing. Once you got an idea like this into your head, you couldn't get it out again; you couldn't just forget about it. At least some part of this idea was going to have to be implemented.

But how? His mind still reeled at that.

He was still standing at the window, his drink untouched, when a car came slowly up the drive, splashing in the puddles. Wendy dashed in a few minutes later, putting her keys and her handbag on the sideboard by the door. 'Hi! Drinking alone?'

'What? No, not really. In fact, I poured it out and then forgot about it. Everything all right? Did you eat?'

'Yes. I had something sent in. How about you?'

'I'm not hungry'

'How did it go with Ian? Did he have anything useful to say?'

'Yes. Of course. We've got to make some fairly tough decisions, about whether to break up certain processes and go for a more decentralised, more focused approach. At least, he says that's what we've got to decide. He made it fairly clear that that's what he thinks we have to do, and that there really isn't much choice.'

'What do you think?'

'I think he may be right. I hate to say it, it would be a lot easier if he were wrong. But I think we need to consider it, at least.'

She sat down on the sofa, quietly. 'I know that your business and mine are vastly different. But I can tell you from my own experience, at the moment, that this kind of thing can work. By working with three or four concentrated units instead of one big, general one, you can achieve greater focus. Of course you need someone to act as coordinator and make sure all the business units, or whatever you want to call them, are driving in the agreed strategic direction, but that's what you would do, or what I would do. We're here to be the boss, to provide direction and make sure other people do what they're meant to do. The style for achieving that may not be as direct, but you need a clear view of what needs to be done.'

'Yes,' he said. 'I can see that. What I'm not sure is that this is the best thing for Wentworth. It sounds attractive, but will it actually work?'

'Can you find out?'

'I shall have to. Tell me what you did to make you so sure this kind of option would work for your business.'

'Some basic analysis of the potential for growth, coupled with some even more basic analysis of the amount of time I could logically spend as the CEO and of how effective I could be. To a certain extent, I'm not worried about levels of profitability, not in the same way you are. I'm worried about the fact that I can't spend the time I want on running the overall business. I get trapped in detail. If I can't get my head above the water, so to speak, and get a better general picture of what's going on, then I'll continue to make sub-optimal decisions, and sooner or later I'm going to make a serious mistake. That's one of the main reasons I'm doing what I'm doing, to improve control, not dilute it.'

He was very tired. He put down the untasted drink and rubbed his eyes. 'So what are you going to do now?'

'That's one of the reasons I was so late tonight. We've got a site in Ottawa, right where I want it near the Parliament buildings. I'm going up next week to start organising things. I'll be gone for about four days.'

'Fine,' he said wearily. 'I suppose it's for the best.'

'For the best? What do you mean?'

'I mean it's what you need to do. Go on and do it then, and good luck.'

There was a long silence. She said, 'Do you resent what I'm

doing, John?'

He turned around suddenly, angered that she should mis-understand him. 'Of course I don't! I resent the fact that I feel unsure and uncertain. And all of this within the constraints of time and expectations to improve overall performance. I'm unsure what I need to do. You're successful at what you do, well, that's good. But don't expect me to lead three hearty cheers on your behalf, not just now.'

She said, levelly, 'I'm going to bed.' He stood there forever, it seemed, aghast at what he had said, listening to her moving about upstairs. Eventually he poured his whisky down the drain, turned out the light and went to bed himself, in silence. The rain was drumming on the roof and on the window, and that was the last sound he heard before he fell asleep.

Chapter 13

"Eventually we need to drive the market instead of being driven by it"

It was a bright spring morning; there was a fresh west wind blowing and the air was warm. It ought to have been the sort of morning when a man felt glad to be alive.

Hart walked into his office and dropped his briefcase on the desk. Then he went back out and poured himself a cup of coffee. He was later than usual; he had not slept well the previous night and had, for the first time since he could remember, slept through the alarm. All the way down the Queen Elizabeth Way his mind had been running steadily on two parallel tracks; on the task in front of him at work and on what he was going to do about his wife.

Darlene Myers came into the office behind him and said good morning. Hart answered her, absently, and returned to his office. He had left several letters from the previous afternoon, and he sat down now to answer these; halfway through the first he realised he had stopped in mid-sentence and was staring into space.

He shook himself and went on to finish the letters as quickly as possible. His mind went back to the meeting where Macallister had told them all bluntly that they had not only been looking at their markets in the wrong way, but had quite possibly been running their factory in the wrong way as well. His generous allowance that they were on the road to sorting things out had not entirely taken the sting out of his comments.

He went into Darlene's office, asked her to type up the letters and came back to his own looking at a report on the pay negotiations which Tim Pringle had just left for him. Pringle had now been with Wentworth for about five years; so had Alan Mills. Nick Moretti had been here longer than that. Tony Leclerc had been marketing director for three years. All of them had an understandable belief that the way they had been managing their particular parts of the company was the correct one; to give them their due, they had made a success of this company for quite some time. No one likes change; and change is even less welcome when you are dealing with a rooted, fixed system like most manufacturing plants. At least marketing types were used to the problems raised by constant flexibility and adaptation, but they fell into the same trap as everyone else in assuming that flexibility ended when you reached the shop floor.

For himself it was different. He was the new broom, intended to sweep clean, and it was both right and necessary that he not be affected by the views of those who had been here before him. And yet, it was equally right that he should have faith in his managers, and he genuinely wanted to believe that they were competent, capable people who had it in them to solve Wentworth's problems. He was certain, at both the emotional and intellectual levels, that they did. That made it all the harder to contradict them and tell them that they were going to have to change some of their most deeply held beliefs.

Not all of them would resist. Shirley Easton had been at Wentworth for several years as well, but she was stepping into a new position and would be eager to put her own stamp on any new strategic direction the company might take. For exactly the opposite reason, Tony Leclerc was unlikely to raise objections, and Leclerc too had a flexible mind, one that was capable of dealing with change and understanding it in a relatively short period of time. Tim Pringle was a man who liked challenges and would probably enjoy reshaping the company purely for the intellectual exercise.

That left Alan Mills and Nick and his managers. These were bright men, but they were men who had also spent as much as two decades learning that cost-cutting and economies of scale were the driving force behind sound management; these were vital principles which had to be met. The dream of manufacturing managers was a large plant to gain economies of scale, coupled with the smallest possible workforce so as to minimise costs as much as possible. Hart could remember from several years ago having a long wrangle with his managing director, who firmly believed that labour costs were crippling the company, even when Hart showed him figures indicating that labour accounted for less than 10 percent of the company's total costs. But people went on investing in more and more labour-saving technology, never bothering to check the impact on business complexity, analyse the costs of managing technology or evaluate overhead costs – even though these costs might be four or five times higher than the costs of labour.

He shook his head; he was wool-gathering again. But if arguments on cost-cutting could be wrong, then so could arguments on economies of scale. He needed something to convince his directors. Wentworth was not currently a spectacularly successful company. But equally it was not unsuccessful either. The decision being contemplated was large. Large enough to push the business one way or the other. And one thing was certain, if they made the changes and undertook the investments then, like most decisions in manufacturing, they would not be rescinded. Companies were rarely prepared to invest a second time.

He could of course simply override them. But that was no way to run a business. Imposing your views on others didn't work in a company, any more than it would work at home.

Darlene brought the letters in for him to sign. He scrawled his signature hastily over his title, *John Hart, Chief Executive Officer*, and stared at the letters for a moment. Darlene said, 'John, is everything all right?'

'What? Oh, yes. Just reflecting on how illegible my signature is becoming.'

'I didn't mean about the letters. I just wondered. . . . You seem to be a little preoccupied this morning. I just wondered if everything was all right, you know, at home.'

Hart looked up at her sharply. 'Everything is fine,' he said firmly. 'This strategy business is bothering me, that's all. Sorry if I'm being a bit vague.'

'No, no, it's all right. I just wanted to make sure you were okay.'

'I'm fine, really. Thanks for asking.'

She hovered in the doorway, not quite sure if she wanted to believe him. 'Can I get you another cup of coffee or something?'

At that he smiled. 'Honestly, Darlene, I'm okay. I appreciate the concern, though. And thanks for the coffee, but I'm off to walk around the plant in a few minutes. Can you hold all my calls?'

'Sure.'

Friendly, cheerful, and competent were all epithets he would have applied to his secretary, but perceptive she was not. If Darlene was noticing, then things must be getting bad. He wondered who else in the building had noticed. Pringle, almost certainly had; he could expect a quiet visit from the personnel manager soon, asking if things were all right and was there anything he needed. Well, he could take that from Tim, but he doubted if he could take it from anyone else.

His mistake, he supposed, had been to think that because they were so similar in outlook and in their goals that it would all work. He had been young when he married the first time, and he and his wife had been obvious opposites in temperament and attitude. People especially her parents, had said hopefully that they balanced each other, and indeed it had seemed to be so for a time. But balance alone was not enough for a marriage; there needed to be some common purpose as well. He thought that with Wendy he had found that. Was it possible that this marriage, too, could founder, not because of differences, but because they were too similar?

Perhaps it was simply foolish to believe that anything would work because it ought to work or was supposed to work. We're used to that. We buy something in a shop, and when it doesn't work right away, we take it back. We get married, and when that doesn't work, we return it to the shop as well. But institutions needed effort to make them work. You had to tackle them on a practical, rather than a theoretical, level and that applied to personal as well as professional institutions. You couldn't do things just because that's how they were supposed to be done.

He left the office a few minutes later for his morning tour, and took some comfort from walking down through the moulding shop between the large presses, seeing the machines and men working together as usual with the morning light coming through the tall, dirty, east windows. There was something solid and reassuring about a place like this. You could see the machines, see the processes in action and see a solid product coming out at the end. You could see what you were doing, see what you were making. Down here you could put your hands on the business and feel it, something which you could not do in the isolation of the office and the boardroom.

Near the door which led to the assembly room he found Nick Moretti and Dave Kochner the foreman, heads together over a piece of paper. Hart discovered that they were discussing how long it would take to set up the machine #10 to do a run of plastic containers which had just been ordered. This particular customer was fond of just-in-time requirements, waiting until the last possible minute to place orders so as to avoid having to hold containers in their own inventory. It was no doubt a practice which the customer found beneficial, but it could play havoc with production schedules.

'Who's the customer?' asked Hart.

'DKW Chemicals,' Moretti said. 'Yeah, that's right, the ones who are giving us trouble on price. That's just great! They come at us from one side asking us to cut price, and then on the other side, they don't do anything to let us make savings. They give us these little bitty orders, and if you ask them if they're going to want a repeat order, they say they don't know.'

'Which means we can't choose the option, should we wish, of making inventory ahead of time and hold it in stock,' Hart said.

'That's expensive too. But it could be a consideration as this is a three hour mould change for a ten hour production run.'

'How often do we deal with this order?'

'Four to six times a year, I'd say. Overall the volume is reasonable. The problem is, the volume on any individual order is low. But DKW only sees the overall annual volume, and that's the basis for setting their pricing policy.'

'The annual volume is high, but the order size is low. You

know, Nick, annual volume doesn't matter. It's the order size that counts, in so far as it impacts our profits.'

Moretti looked up. 'Sure. But if you don't get the overall volumes, you don't show a profit at year-end, no matter how profitable your individual batches might be.'

'Yes, but from your point of view, from the manufacturing point of view, overall volume is of secondary importance. You could have two products with a volume of a hundred thousand a year, but if one of them is done as one production run and the other is done as six production runs scattered through the production year, which one is the most work? Which one costs the most to produce?'

Dave Kochner had begun to actually pay attention and look interested. Hart turned to him. 'You play two hockey games, Dave, and you win one of them one-nil and the other one six-five. Which one have you had to work hardest to win?'

'Probably the second one,' said Kochner. 'But it's all the same in the end, you've still won.'

'Okay, maybe it's a bad analogy. But which one of these orders do you think makes the most work?'

Kochner glanced sidelong at his boss. He said self-consciously, 'We would do more work on the second order.'

'Yes not only is there a cost factor every time we have to stop work and set up for a new order, but it focuses the problem more sharply. We're finally at the point where we can track products by behaviour, and hence by cost, on a regular, individual basis. I also think we can finally begin defining products by groups according to behaviour. The manufacturing task to support low-volume, short customer lead time products, for instance, is very different to that of supporting high-volume call-offs on a scheduled basis. Trying to meet both through the same manufacturing set-up governed by the same costing system and measured on the same performance criteria means that some markets are less well-aligned than others. Also, what do you concentrate on in manufacturing? Reducing set-ups so as to meet the needs of one set of customers, or fine tune the system to control and reduce costs to meet the different needs of another set.

'What do you think, Nick, now that you've had time to mull it over? Suppose you had two separate production units, one of which dealt with the orders you do six times a year and the other dealing with the ones you do once a year. Could you not get efficiencies out of that?'

'Yes. The six times a year line would have higher costs.'

'And we'd charge correspondingly higher prices. The trouble with DKW,' said Hart, 'is not the price they want to pay, but the volume they want to order.'

He discussed the same rationale with Shirley Easton at lunch time, and she nodded. 'Well, it's one or the other, isn't it? Order more, and it becomes worth our while to make the product at that price. Either that, or . . . Or what?'

'Either pay the present price, increase the order to make the demanded price economical or look for another supplier. I know that the Eleventh Commandment is, 'Thou shalt not turn away business.' But if we're going to make this strategy work, we're going to have to be in charge of our own strategic decisions. There's no point in deciding to concentrate on the kinds of business that will make us money and then taking on customers whose orders yield little or no profit.'

'You're right,' said Easton, 'though I get a kind of funny feeling in my stomach when I think about telling a customer to take a hike.'

'It's something we'll have to start thinking about. I believe we'll find that under our new regime, not every customer is a good customer. We, and that particularly means you, will have to start thinking about how we want to direct our marketing effort to keep it in line with our manufacturing focus, or equally, about which attractive markets you wish to develop and what that means to manufacturing in terms of its strategic response.'

'Sure,' said Easton. 'Eventually, we need to be driving the market instead of being driven by it.'

'Exactly,' said Hart. He went back to his office, confident that at least one of his managers was thinking the same way.

He went home that night on his own; Wendy was in Ottawa. He did not want to think about that.

After dinner he sat down in the living room with the television on, but the volume turned down; there was a nature programme on with pictures of African wildlife providing an occasional distraction. He thought, how many times have I done this in times past, come home, eaten dinner and gone straight back to work again?

The business at hand was simple; given that he wanted to introduce the concepts of focused manufacturing to Wentworth, what were the areas of focus to be?

He had in front of him Shirley Easton's charts of her survey of orders, and he read these again, slowly, while the television-screen lions prowled across the savannah and pursued unsuccessfully some form of antelope. In the end he leaned back thinking things through.

The simplest way of dividing the products seems to be to split them three ways. First, there are the high-volume orders which – let's be careful here – involve large production runs. We'll call these Category A. Then there are the orders which are low-volume, but which occur frequently, thus leading, as Nick suggested, to high annual volumes. These low-volume order products are frequently ones where high quality standards are set, particularly with regard to hygiene for our food and cosmetics customers. These we shall call Category C. Last, there are the orders which fall between the two with low to moderate volumes, often for fairly complex products. We shall call these Category B products.

By the nature of its products, Wentworth was a batch manufacturer; it managed repeat production runs. However, the volume range of its orders was very wide and covered low through high volume. The task, it appeared, was to enhance the company's capabilities to deal with these differences.

Well, why not? Take Category A products, separate them out into a separate unit, and build a high-volume capability. Take Category C products, and put them into something that reflects their low-volume nature. And Category B we'll organise between the two.

He picked up a piece of paper and began writing quickly, trying to see if everything he knew so far would support such a division of products. In the end he had a rough table which laid out the marketing and manufacturing differences between the product categories. The point now was to make those differences work for, rather than against, the company. If we can exploit the differences, he thought, rather than the similarities between these products, then we shall indeed be getting somewhere.

Shirley Easton had said it gave her a funny feeling. Hart knew what she meant. All of this went so much against his experience and business principles.

Of course, splitting the company into focused units did not in itself provide all the answers. There was a very real danger, unless the transition was handled carefully, that they would end up not improving the situation, or even making it worse. And Hart could not get out of his mind that this was essentially a defensive measure, a response to market demands rather than a proactive attempt to take control. It all resembled the British army at Waterloo, forming squares and standing back to back to stand off Napoleon's cavalry.

That might be one way of looking at the problem, but Hart had always been dubious about analogies of business and warfare. In fact, Wentworth and its customers had something in common; they both needed the business for their own reasons, the customers for supply, Wentworth for profit. It made far more sense to try and ensure that relations between the two parties were sound and remained tied to each other in terms of need and provision. Thus, while a manufacturing reorganisation might indeed be a defensive measure, a re-shaping of the company was distinctly proactive, an attempt to become both more responsive to the needs of customers and more aggressive in developing new business in prime areas of interest – Categories A, B and C.

The wildlife programme had come to an end, and the news was on. He turned up the volume on the remote control, thinking that the idea about reshaping the company could wait for another day; it was enough to have gotten this far. The news led with an item from Ottawa, and while the reporter's voice droned on there was a background shot of Parliament Hill. Then, for some reason, another of a nearby shopping area. In one corner of the screen, he fancied he could see a 'For Sale' sign in the window of a shop. He thought, I wonder if that's the one Wendy's after?

Suddenly he felt quite ashamed of himself. She was launching one of the biggest ventures of her life, and all he had been able to do so far was tell her he thought she was wrong. And when she had rejected his judgement, he had become resentful.

What he had said to Darlene Myers was quite true; the problems of Wentworth *were* getting to him. And he was indeed letting the theoretical side of the problem dominate the practice. There was absolutely nothing wrong between them that a little practical application couldn't cure.

A sudden resolve came to him. I'll fly up tomorrow afternoon and see her. If I leave the office by 3:30, I can be in Ottawa in time for dinner. The first flight in the morning won't get me back in the office until late, and I can't afford to play hookey for too long, but I could take the last flight back at night. It was all quite illogical, quite unnecessary, and just the sort of foolish, impulsive behaviour which John Hart normally deplored. But he felt that he wanted to see her, to talk to her, and that the telephone wouldn't do. And, there was a fear that if he left it

185

until she came home, it might be too late.

He was tired, and he went to bed soon after and slept soundly without dreaming. He arrived at the office early the next morning and booked the flight himself. He was in such good humour by the time Darlene Myers arrived that the secretary shrugged and decided she had indeed made a mistake the previous day. Hart came through at 9:15 and handed her a good copy of the notes he had made the night before. 'Get these typed up as soon as you can, will you? I'm going off a little after 3:00 today, and I'd like Nick to see these before I go.'

'Nick's not in,' she said. 'Graham Carter just rang through from the assembly room to say they've got a message that he's got the flu. He'll try to be in tomorrow.'

'Oh, blast.' He thought for a moment. 'Okay. Get them typed up and put them in his in-box, then. All right, I'm going to go and walk around the shop. I should be back in half an hour.'

For a change, the tour of the factory produced not even minor issues, and Hart reflected that despite Moretti's absence everything was running smoothly; it was a tribute to Nick that the men under him knew exactly what was expected of them. He thought, this is a good business. We're going to make something of it.

In the same mood of optimism, he left the office carrying only his briefcase and drove to the airport. The flight to Ottawa was uneventful, the plane flying through gloriously clear air in the late afternoon and coming down to land in the early evening. He came out of the airport feeling slightly embarrassed at his own behaviour and took a taxi into the city. The taxi let him off outside the hotel, and he paid the driver and walked inside.

The girl at the desk offered to phone the room for him, and he waited while she let the phone ring several times. 'There's no answer, sir, but she has taken her key. Perhaps she's in the bar or the coffee shop?'

'Thanks, I'll try the bar. If she's not there, I'll come back and leave a message.'

He walked through to the bar and looked around. The light

was dim, as it always was in hotel lounges, and there was some sort of piped-in piano music coming from the shadowy ceiling. Apart from the waiter there were only half a dozen people in the room; he had to strain to see that one of two people at the corner table was in fact Wendy.

Across from her, just raising his hand to order another drink, was Ian Macallister.

Chapter 14

"We've got to apply focus to the whole company, but only if it fits"

Afterwards, he was chiefly to remember the incident by the initial silence; one of the most awkward silences he'd ever encountered. The fact that the awkwardness was all his only made matters worse.

'Hello,' he said to Macallister, coming forward. 'I didn't expect to see you here.'

'Likewise,' said Macallister. 'Well, sit down. Can I get you a drink?'

His voice sounded natural, but his manner was puzzled, though not alarmed. Hart looked from his wife to his friend and back again. Wendy said rather sharply, 'John? Is something wrong at home?'

'No. No, should there be?'

'I . . . You didn't phone or anything. I had no idea you were coming.'

No, thought Hart, you didn't. Was it his imagination, or was Wendy looking more than usually pretty tonight? She had dark eyes which could be very expressive and they were being expressive now; they were telling him, warningly, that there had better be an explanation for what was happening.

'I thought I'd surprise you,' he said. 'What brings you up to Ottawa, Ian?'

'I had to spend a couple of days with my difficult client, the paper company. I'm just on my way back to Montreal tonight. In fact my plane leaves pretty soon, so if I could buy you two lovely people a drink, I'll be on my way. How are things going down your way, John?'

'I hope to have something for you by the beginning of next week. Can I give you a call on Monday?'

'I'm out Monday morning, but give me a call after lunch. Right, kids, I'm off. Nice to see you again, Wendy, and best of luck with the shop. Bye.'

'Goodbye,' said Hart, without regret. 'Talk to you on Monday.'

Macallister left, with just a hint of amusement in his face as he turned at the door of the lounge to wave goodbye. Hart sat down, looking first at the glass of beer which Macallister had bought him and then at his wife. 'What on earth was he doing here?'

'Like he said, he was seeing a client. He's been in the hotel for the last two days, and we only just bumped into each other this evening. John! Do you honestly think that he and I. . . .'

Although the idea had certainly leaped to mind, he didn't honestly believe it, he put on his best serious expression and said, 'It's always the way, isn't it? A man's wife and his best friend, the people he trusts most in the world. It's tragic, really, when you stop and think about it.'

She burst out laughing. 'You idiot! What *are* you doing here? You're the only one of the three of us without a decent excuse. Are you spying on me?'

'Yes, I was going to hide in the shadows and watch you, but you spotted me. How are you? How is the shop going?'

'Did you come up here just to ask me that?'

'Yes, and to buy you dinner.'

She looked at him, smiling, as if she was making up her mind. 'The shop is going fine. I closed the deal for the property yesterday, and I spent today talking to artists and to potential suppliers. It's going well.'

'Find anything good?'

'Yes, I did. I've got some samples up in my room. Do you want to come and see?'

'Yes, I'd like to. Then, let's go and have some dinner.'

'This is quite a modern hotel,' Wendy said, smiling. 'We could probably order room service, if you like.'

He paused. 'Is this going on your expense account, or mine?'

'Oh, that *is* romantic,' she said. 'Next you'll be telling me we have to eat early because you're flying back to Toronto tonight. You're not?'

'I should. Really. I cut out early this afternoon, and I can't really afford to be late tomorrow.'

'Why, will Darlene give you a black mark? John Hart, do you really mean to say that you're such an inadequate CEO that the company will collapse without your presence for a few hours? Will it really?'

Moretti had been absent all day and nothing had happened. He hesitated for just a second. 'No,' he said, 'I don't suppose it will. All right. Lead the way.'

They stood up together, and their eyes met, and Hart knew then that he had done the right thing. Such a seemingly complicated problem; such a simple and obvious solution. He took his wife's hand and they walked to the elevator.

Back in the office about 11:00 the next morning, Hart picked up the phone and rang Nick Moretti. The production director answered on the third ring.

'Nick, how are you feeling? How's the flu?'

'A little groggy,' Moretti said indistinctly. 'However, I felt I should put in an appearance. I got your notes from yesterday. They look very interesting.'

Hart, who had arrived at the office with renewed enthusiasm and resolve, realised that Nick would not be up to much today. 'Do you want to leave this until later, Nick? If you're not 100 percent, you've probably got enough on your plate at the moment.'

'No, it's all right. Maybe I'm hallucinating from too many decongestant pills, but I think I've got some ideas. I'd like to talk some of these things through before too much more time passes. I've got a meeting with Tim in about five minutes, but can I stagger along and see you afterwards?'

'Yes, do.' He put the phone down, wondering what had led to this change of heart.

He was on the telephone again when Moretti came in and sat down holding a sheaf of papers. 'That was our friend Clarkson from Conway Foods,' said Hart as soon as he was off the telephone. 'It seems they are definitely going ahead with this cook chill foods venture, and he wanted to be reassured that we could cope with his business. I took the liberty of saying that we could. Have you seen the new product specifications they sent over last week?'

'Yeah, I was looking at them again this morning. Trying to figure out where these orders would fit in your suggested focused units.'

'What did you think of the idea of separating products/orders into focused units? Can it be done?'

'Sure, it can be done. But you made a note here that you are worried about duplication of effort, of creating plants within plants that still have the same focus problems as the old plant had, and I think there's a danger of that. If we get this wrong we could well end up by reducing effective capacity, at a time when capacity is already at a premium.'

Hart nodded; this was his own worry exactly. Moretti went on, 'Why not follow the original logic, and divide the production facilities according to products classified by order-winners?'

Hart looked up. 'I'm not sure I'm with you.'

'Well, I may be splitting hairs, but it seems to me there's more ways of grouping orders than just by volume. One is by the nature of the product in terms of its end use and by customer, which is more or less equivalent to the marketing logic we were using. The second is by the nature of the process, which is what you've done here. The third is by order-winners, the things we've been discussing all along. I can see ways of segmenting products by lead time/delivery speed, or by price, and the implication for low cost, although price sensitivity is often connected to volume. If we use these types of criteria as the basis for segmentation, we would, in theory, find that we are grouping production according to the factors which make our products successful, and, in turn, what manufacturing has to become good at, rather than those criteria which govern the way the product is made. I think there may be other factors still which govern the way we segment the products, and I think we've got to make sure we've thought of them all and discussed them all.'

193

Hart, who had been bracing himself for objections, stared at his production director. 'Yes. Yes, you're quite right. I think I got the issue of volume rather too fixed in my mind. In fact, the same three categories still work, but the way we allocate products to different production units might change.'

'Yeah, I think it would. Where it might make a difference, too, is in how we switch products from one unit to another. That's what's been worrying me about these Conway Foods orders. We've got, what, six different products which will vary in terms of subsequent orders and size of repeat orders. Which product category are they? But if we assume that category B means products which are sold on the basis of quick delivery, and Category C means products which are sold on the basis of technical capability, then we can see that the initial orders are going to be for Category C, but repeat business once the customer gets his own production up and running will switch to Category B, and, in some instances, it could be Category A. Am I making sense?'

'Absolutely.'

'Well; that's something to be thankful for. I'm not against a product switching from one focused unit to another, but I think it's important we know where we start from and what the rationale is.'

'That sounds logical as well. But, if we pick one of these Conway Foods products, for example, we've got a number of order-winners. Quality, delivery and price.'

'Ah. But let's take it order by order, shall we? For the *first* order, they want a design that works and our technical capability provides that. But we don't know what will be required of us other than the hygiene standards. And the price is extremely generous. We can afford to spend some time and get it absolutely right. Once we get going, if Shirley's reasoning and analysis is right, things are going to happen in the product life-cycle. The emphasis on factors such as price and delivery speed is going to change. So the first production unit concentrates on getting small orders right the first time. The second unit would concentrate on producing larger and repeat orders on a more cost-efficient basis and with an emphasis on quality and delivery while the third unit would work on large-scale orders where price is the primary consideration. Equally, products for which demand does not increase over time may well stay within the first production unit.'

'Now, supposing Conway Foods has a rush of blood to the head and decides to order in a lot of stock and hold a big inventory instead of having us deliver just in time. We'd switch from the second unit to the third. We've got to think of some names for these things too, what with the second unit and Category B, I'm getting confused. Or that could just be the antihistamines.'

'No, I think that's necessary. We shall have to call them something at some stage. Can you take this forward from here? We still are working on the details. Would you link with Shirley's analysis and together come to some agreement about the way our markets split. In some instances, remember, the split may not be tidy. Once you have a feel for that, could you then outline the kind of manufacturing changes and engineering changes you would need to make. An overview of the latter is all that's needed at this stage. Something for us to begin to address the issues involved.'

'I can,' said Moretti. 'But if you don't mind, I want to make some recommendations about other changes as well. What we're facing, if we go ahead with this focus plan, is a very major loss of manufacturing economies of scale. I have to tell you I am very concerned about that. For one thing, at present we are discussing only the breakup of the manufacturing plant; the rest of the company stays as it is. Well, I can see all sorts of problems with that. There's a very real danger of putting focus into the manufacturing side, but not considering it elsewhere in the company. If I understand what your friend Macallister said, then we've got to put focus into the whole company if we're to see any benefit.'

'We're basing this change on the belief that markets are no

longer similar in terms of behaviour,' Hart said. 'That has repercussions for the whole business, I agree. I think we can get too worried about economies of scale. They are, as a general rule, a very sound basis for organising a business, provided the business merits their use. The only real rule in this sort of situation is, do what works. And if we can make more profit by withdrawing from economies of scale and moving into focused manufacturing which costs more, but earns more yet, then we will be justified.'

Moretti nodded. 'The one thing I have been opposed to from the start is the myth of panaceas. "Just-In-Time," "Total Quality Management," I've seen 'em all. and they've all got some benefits to provide, no doubt about it, but they're not cure-alls. I was worried that any strategic solution we tried to apply here would be of a similar nature, and when Macallister proposed breaking up the plant, well, my heart sank. I thought, here's another one, another quick-fix solution to a complicated problem, you know?'

'What made you change your mind?'

'Just simple reflection, running over what Shirley, you and Ian himself said. It does make sense, in today's markets. I think it's worth a try. I just hope we can do it.'

'Well, if we're all agreed on what we want to do, then we can, I'm sure of that. We're all committted, and Ian will remain on hand to consult and advise. We will need to start thinking about implementation quite soon, however, if we're going to put something before Laurentian.'

He leaned back in his chair. 'I can't believe I'm saying this. We're actually talking not about what we're going to do, but how we're going to do it.'

'That's still a pretty big question,' Moretti warned. 'There's still three questions to be dealt with. First, I have to figure out how I want to organise the manufacturing plant in order to align it with the markets. Then we have to figure out how the infrastructure will need to be organised to support the manu-facturing units and provide the necessary support for the markets. Finally, we have to decide on the level of investment we need in order to meet market demand. *And*, we have to take into account the fact that these questions are all linked. For instance, there must be business targets for all of our business units, and we have to agree on these before we decide on the size and structure of each business unit, the market plan and the level of required investment.'

'Yes. Well, as I see it, it's your task to sort out the organisation of the manufacturing plant, and how you'll handle things like scheduling and quality control, maintenance and tool rooms. Tony's and Shirley's task is to decide how the marketing department should support the focus concepts, and that will include things such as estimating and re-orienting the sales reps in the field. What I am going to do is ask all of you to write a report for me on what you believe is possible and where you think the company's best interests lie. I will then set our goals accordingly, and instruct you to prepare your final plans. I'll get Darlene to put out a memo to that effect. Okay?'

It was late in the day and Hart was just beginning to clear his desk when the telephone rang. Darlene said, 'John, it's Mike Connors on the line.'

'Hello, John,' Connors said. 'How are you all doing up there?'

'Very well, I think. We're onto quite a good piece of business with one of our big customers who is developing some new products, and it looks like it ought to go on into the long term.'

'Making yourself indispensable, are you? That's the stuff.' Connors had a habit, Hart had learned by now, of not actually telling you why he had called, but just listening to you talk until he had learned what he wanted to know. Taking a guess now, Hart said, 'I assume you called because you want to know about our strategic proposals.'

'Well, I hadn't heard from you for a while, so I thought I'd just call and pass the time of day,' Connors said easily. 'Have you got anything new to tell me, or should I wait and call another day?'

'As it happens, you're in luck, I was going to write to you, but I may as well outline what we're going to do. Basically, we want to focus our manufacturing effort on some key areas of activity, so that our production supports the demands of our markets. Doing that is going to require that we restructure the company fairly extensively, and that we invest in some key areas where we currently lack capacity.'

'That sounds interesting,' said Connors. 'What kind of restructuring are you looking at?'

'We intend to split the company into two or three different business units, each focusing on a particular type of market. It'll mean some overhead increases, but it will also mean more flexibility and more opportunities to respond to changes in market conditions.'

'Uh-huh,' said Connors. 'And then what?'

'That I can't tell you, not yet.' Hart took a deep breath, looked at his desk calendar and committed himself. 'In three weeks, however, I will be able to tell you what our targets are and what level of investment we will need. Can I present something to you then?'

'Sure you can,' said Connors. 'In fact, I think you'd better fly on down here and present it to us in person. Do you want to do that? How about the 30th of the month, then?'

'The 30th it is. Let me know the time and place, will you?'

'I'll get my secretary to send all the details to Darlene. John, I really do think this sounds interesting. We'll look forward to hearing what you've got to say.'

After the call was over Hart sat down at his desk again for a moment, feeling unaccountably nervous. Connors had been satisfied, even encouraging. Why should he be worrying now?

After a moment it came to him that he was nervous because he had not only staked his own professional reputation on this plan, but he had persuaded his colleagues to do likewise. Failure to persuade Laurentian now would be to let them all down.

But he had to persuade them. He knew, knew beyond all doubt, that this was the right thing to do and that only a radical change could shake Wentworth out of its rut and put it back on course for growth and success. All he had to do now was persuade the people who actually owned the company.

Chapter 15

"Being market-driven"

Later, looking back on those three weeks, Hart found he could remember very few details about what had actually happened. The daily routine of the company was getting steadily busier. Whether it was because of some long ago initiatives on the part of the sales reps or because the marketing department had been fired up by the prospect of change and were communicating their enthusiasm to their customers, orders were coming in steadily. DKW Chemicals did indeed decide to take their business elsewhere, and Hart had a cold moment when Tony Leclerc passed on the news, but the new Conway business and new business from Excalibur would more than offset the loss in terms of both volume and profits.

'We can use the very fact of the reorganisation as a marketing advantage,' said Leclerc. 'We can present the focus concept to customers, and use it to reassure them that we can meet their needs. That's a spin-off benefit we hadn't thought about at first.'

Leclerc was practically clearing his desk by now, handing over to Shirley Easton; his last day with the firm was to be the day before Hart left for the meeting with Laurentian. He looked rather wistful at times as he saw what he was going to be missing. 'I spoke to Mike Connors the other day,' he said. 'He asked me if I was going to want to introduce focused manufacturing in my company as soon as I took over. I think he's expecting it to spread like an epidemic.'

'Iam Macallister would tell him that it should,' Hart said. 'Ian thinks manufacturing in Western countries is markedly out of date and out of touch, and that all attempts at reform to date have been on the basis of panacea solutions. I'm tempted to bring him with me to Philadelphia.' In fact, Hart was asking Macallister to look at his presentation before he wrote the final draft.

His first conversation with Macallister after returning from Ottawa was an embarrassing moment that stuck in his memory. 'Look,' Hart had said, 'I'm sorry about that incident at the hotel. I really should have let Wendy know I was coming up.'

'Thought you'd catch her with the other man, did you? Well, you got us all right. I half expected to see a camera man behind you with popping flashbulbs.'

'All right, all right. You don't need to keep rubbing it in. I've got a question for you. We're committed now to the focus principle, and I think we're looking at three different manufacturing units. How much sense does it make to divide our marketing, finance and personnel departments among the three units as well?'

'Well, there's the classic trade-off in these sorts of situations. In some, it is better for a business to leave some functions on a centralised basis. You need to be aware of the danger of treating the concept of focus as a dogma in the same way as that of economies of scale. The key is, what makes most sense? Also, it is important to recognise that some tasks within an existing function are better allocated and some are better centralised. For example, quality assurance and the laboratory support you have in this plant is typically better provided on a centralised basis, whereas quality control, the actual checking procedures, are better done at the point of manufacture inside each unit. Experience has shown that the best way forward is to allocate those tasks over which there is little doubt. As focus should be approached as an evolutionary process, so other functions can be reviewed in the future. Hold off on the decision until then.'

'That makes sense. I can see how that will help us determine our initial step.'

'How long have you got before you make the presentation?'

'Less than three weeks.'

'Whew. That close.' Macallister asked several questions about the manufacturing units and then said, 'Put it this way. Manufacturing processes are your hardware, support functions and systems are your software. You set up the hardware the way you want it. The advantages of tailoring your infrastructure to the manufacturing requirements, instead of vice versa, ought to be fairly obvious, but be careful you don't end up fixing things that ain't broke. You need to look at each part of your infrastructure and decide whether or not it will support your manufacturing effort better if you split it up, and if it won't, don't. By the way, how are your own managers taking to this?'

'Tim Pringle from personnel is enthusiastic. He's been convinced from the start that orienting parts of the business to specific markets will yield substantial benefits. Alan Mills is less certain. He's argued a very persuasive case for retaining some centralised functions but he has suggested we allocate the management accounting role to each unit and to provide decentralised financial management for each unit from the centre. Responsibility will rest with each focused unit, but he feels that overall control may stay centralised. I think he's right in our case.'

'That's the important part. If it seems to be the right thing to do, do it. It all sounds a bit like psycho-analysis, but in fact it's just being practical. I would certainly strongly favour that goal-setting be the province of an attenuated central management group. One thing you will have to beware of in the future is that business units have a tendency to wander off and set goals of their own, regardless of where the company should be going. You need to keep their eyes on the ball, and you will have to demonstrate to your parent that you can control them.'

'Yes. Here again, I think financial controls are important. Financial planning as well as marketing planning will be driven from the very top. As well as our formal board of directors, I'm setting up an executive committee of Shirley, Nick, Alan and myself, and the four of us will initiate planning rather than simply approving final plans. I think we can manage the control side.'

He had sounded very confident on the telephone to Macallister. Later, driving home, he was a little surprised to find that he still felt the same way.

After several false starts, summer was definitely coming; the days were longer and the air was genuinely warm. The National Hockey League playoffs had arrived, and attention on the shop floor was focused almost exclusively on how the Toronto Maple Leafs would fare in their playoff series. Only the directors seemed nearly immune; they had their own end game to play.

There were hudnreds of details to be settled. How could the physical reorganisation of the plant be effected with the least difficulty? How should the moulding machines be grouped? How much machine capacity was going to be needed for each business unit, as opposed to the capacity available now? What was the effect likely to be on shift patterns? Should any areas run on a four-shift rather than three-shift format? How would office and work space have to be organised? What additional process capacity was going to be needed to make all three units functional? What additional overhead costs were going to be incurred?

'These unit-based accountancy roles are going to be tricky,' said Alan Mills thoughtfully. 'It is quite possible that they will be seen as some sort of commissar, sent in to keep order and force them all to toe the financial line. Or as someone who will report back everything they say. On the other hand, it is quite possible that they could start working against the interests of the central department.'

'Will it be a problem,' asked Hart, 'if the individual financial goals of the business units are harmonised with the overall financial goals? Surely it's up to us to make sure there is no conflict and that the business units see their way forward. I can see them actually being helpful advisors.'

Nick Moretti nodded. 'Get 'em away from just being budget controllers and actually give them a communications and planning role. They'll probably enjoy having a more diverse job. I know I would if I were one. What did you say earlier, John, about getting away from functional constraints?'

John Hart smiled. 'Absolutely. There's no need that because people have a particular job title that they must only do related tasks. Okay. What's next?'

As they had begun months before with markets and marketing, so they came back to them in the end. 'One of the minor frustrations of being in a company like this is that there are definite limits to how we can influence the markets,' said Tony Leclerc. 'It's not like we can invent a new product and then go out and stimulate market demand for it. There are limits to invention in this business. At present, there are no indications that people are not satisfied with our technical support for the product or that there is any way in which a new product could improve on the benefits these containers offer. However, we must make sure we keep an open mind on future possibilities.'

Shirley Easton looked up. 'For the moment, I think there's enough room for manoeuvre within the markets we already have to keep us busy, without needing to invent new ones.'

'True,' said Hart. 'But what are we going to do about our existing markets? How are we going to approach them? And how are we going to ensure that the business we get is the right business? I foresee some fairly rocky times ahead with our sales people.'

'That's certainly true,' said Easton. 'They've been brought up from birth to believe that any customer is a good customer, and the idea of turning business down isn't going to sit too well with one or two of them. We've got to ensure that they are on our side as well. I suspect this is going to mean much tighter sales planning and control than ever before. Traditionally, our sales people have wandered around on their own and have done things their own way, and, so long as business came in, we've never complained. But that will clearly have to be modified.'

'You're right about planning,' said Hart, 'but what are you going to plan for? We're going to set targets for the company as a whole and then break those down for the business units. How will you direct your marketing effort to meet those targets? I really don't think we can expect the sales department to decentralise; the idea of having three different salesmen covering the same patch, or a salesman who is only allowed to take high-volume orders, is not realistic.'

'I think that's right,' said Easton. 'I also don't think it's realistic to set targets for the number of orders or numbers of customers for each business unit, not at this stage. Expectations, yes, and an assumption as to what proportion of overall revenue and profit will be derived from each unit, based on forecasts; those we can do. But when John McTavish goes to visit a new client, we can't know beforehand what the order volume or the other parameters will be, or whether this will be one-off or repeat business. We can guess, from the nature of the company, but guessing isn't the same as knowing.'

'No.' This was Moretti chiming in. 'And we've got too many products whose behaviour doesn't conform to expectations to lead us into that trap again. All right. We have an overall business target for the year ahead. We have an assumption that 20 percent of this sales revenue will be generated by the custom and small orders unit, 30 percent by the mid-volume, high-quality unit, and 50 percent by the large-volume unit. That's gross revenue, not profits. We know that present business levels are about 20 percent below what we'd like them to be. That's 20 percent of 20 percent, 20 percent of the 30 percent and so on. We obviously can and will take any business that is offered to us and count it as a windfall. But in planning terms, we ought to be directing our reps to concentrate on companies where there is potential for new orders of the kind we require.

'Now that may well mean from the reps' point of view that they segment customers by the type of business they do just as they've been doing all along. McTavish might well say, we need more large-volume orders, so I'll go and hit up some chemical companies for the business. And if instead, they offer some custom and small orders, then we take it, say thank you very much, and move on to some more target companies. But what we will be providing for the sales force is more direction, more focus and more support. That ought to improve their business and make their lives easier.'

There was a little silence. 'You're wasted in production,' said

Tony Leclerc. 'You should be in marketing.'
  Moretti just smiled.

A rationale for change, an overall goal, a summary of the focus
to be adopted, detailed goals for each of the three business
units, a summary of the controls to be implemented and a target
figure for investment and production – Hart ticked them all off
mentally as he prepared his case. The penultimate draft went
off to Ian Macallister by fax and was returned the following day
covered in black ink. Most of the queries, however, dealt with
things the directors had already discussed among themselves
and had either worked out or left out purposely as irrelevant. A
greal deal of pragmatism crept in during the final week, with
people going around checking issues and asking, 'Do we *really*
need to worry about this?' Previously there had been a tendency to argue every theoretical point and only then stop to
check and see if it mattered.

  Wendy read the final draft through, nodding occasionally.
'This is a good outline,' she said. 'If I were on Laurentian's
board, I would have a lot of questions to ask you, but I presume
you're allowing for that. I appreciate your worries about main-
taining central control. From my own perspective, I can already
admit it is a lot harder to control three horses than one, harder
than I had thought it would be. The advantages are that I now
have more time to do the controlling, and I control through
asking how suggested developments or known problems impact
the market. I can then leave the day-to-day stuff for each unit to
manage. Controlling through strategy is giving me a tight grip
and reinforces agreed direction. As a consequence, the key
issues are defined more clearly in my own mind. I'm no longer
pulled in all directions at once. I'm able to focus on different
sets of issues with the different businesses. And because of that,
I am better able to exercise appropriate and sound controls.
And even more important still, I'm no longer working 14-hour
days.'

That was certainly true. Apart from the fact that she was up and down to Ottawa almost weekly, Wendy was spending less time in the office and more time in the field. She was also coming home earlier in the evening, and twice in the past week, she had been home before Hart. Already she looked more relaxed and less tired. 'And it's working,' Hart said.

'I'm keeping my fingers crossed,' she said.

'For both of us, I hope.'

She smiled. 'Aren't you happy you decided to pick up the phone way back in March and call Ian? From where I'm sitting, I'd say you owe him quite a lot.'

'I do. He has the precious advantage of detachment and uses it well. I could not have done that without outside help. We are all sceptical at times about consultants and advisors, and there's some that deserve it especially the ones that come in and try to impose quick-fix solutions without ever bothering to know the business.'

'What will you do now? I mean, assuming Laurentian agrees to what you've proposed and lets you have the investment you need? Then what?'

'Well, there's certainly no lying back and taking it easy. Then we have to actually *do* all the things we've said we're going to do, and that is going to take a lot of time and energy over the next several months. But along with the implementation should come the first signs of success, if you like, the first signals from the marketplace that we're doing the right things and making the right moves. If business continues to grow and profits start to grow again, then we'll know. After that. . . .'

He stood by the living room window looking out across the sunlit fields to the south, and after a moment Wendy got up and, standing beside him took his arm. 'After that, who can really say? The processes we've started here will never really end, of course. We'll have to keep constantly monitoring what's going on in the markets and deciding what our next response should be. The situation we're in this year may be quite different next year, and we may find ourselves having to shift the emphasis of the business in order to respond. But what we've done now, I think, is build a framework which will allow us to respond. We've untied our own hands which will help us find an answer to the questions the market poses.'

He returned to the same theme a few days later at the party for Tony Leclerc. The party itself was in the boardroom and was attended by nearly all the office staff and some of the workers from the various manufacturing areas. Leclerc was a popular man. Hart stood up to pay tribute to him and to officially welcome Shirley Easton to her new job. He had also decided to use the occasion to publicise the plans on which they had worked for so long.

'If Laurentian accepts this, there will be a lot of changes in Wentworth,' he said to the ring of faces. 'Some of you may find that your job descriptions, and your jobs themselves, will change quite a lot. You may find you are given new responsibilities, some of which will be quite unfamiliar to you. Some of you may find that you are asked to do things which do not match up with what you perceive your role in this company to be. Some of you may conclude that, as a result, we have lost our minds.'

There was quiet laughter, but most in the room were taking this seriously. Rumours must have been going around for some time now, especially among those who had not been directly consulted. 'Let me assure you,' Hart went on, 'that far from losing our sanity, we have, in fact, been taking a realistic look at this company and its chances for the future. We have concluded that its chances are excellent. But in order to make the most of those chances, we have to adapt so that we are ready for them. We have to be able to meet whatever our markets demand. At the moment this company is highly efficient, but insufficiently flexible. Well, we're going to compromise, just a little, on some aspects of efficiency so that we can become a great deal more flexible.

Flexibility doesn't just come from organisation. It also comes from flexible thinking on the part of the people who work here. I and the other directors will do our best in the weeks ahead to make sure that you are kept in touch with the changes as they happen. At the same time, we expect you to understand that we have reasons for the things we do, and we ask you to make the extra effort to make those changes work.

'You may work for marketing, or in accounts, or on the production line, but you are all part of Wentworth. We're all part of the same team, just as forwards, defencemen and the goaltender are in hockey. Defencemen can score goals, and forwards can prevent them. Well, from now on, we're going to be the same. All working together. I don't want to hear anyone saying "that's not my job." If you work for Wentworth, then it *is* your job. What I want to hear instead is, "Here is a problem. What can I do about it?"

'Okay, I've shot my mouth off long enough. Thanks for listening to me, and enjoy the party.'

'Ask not what your company can do for you, but what you can do for your company,' said Shirley Easton a little later.

'Why not?' said Tony Leclerc. 'It's not a bad philosophy. I don't think we can ever emulate the Japanese philosophy of loyalty to the company, and I'm not sure we want to try. But there's a lot more satisfaction to be gained from construction rather than obstruction.'

'You think so, and I think so,' said Easton, 'but will everyone else think so?'

Leclerc laughed. 'You'll have plenty of time to find out, Shirl. Good luck. And I hope you don't need too much of it.'

Chapter 16

"Adapt or die"

In Philadelphia it was warm and sunny. There was a driver from Laurentian waiting at the airport. He had been to Philadelphia before, always on business, and he knew the way well; he sat in the back of the car and watched the tall glass buildings of the city slide by, impatient to be at his destination.

At the 40-storey building where Laurentian had their head offices, he walked in the front door, briefcase in one hand, overcoat slung over his shoulder. He signed his name in the security guard's book and waited while Mike Connors' secretary came down to collect him. Connors himself, a tall, balding man in his early fifties who looked completely unlike his voice, was in his 15th-storey office. He came around from behind his desk to shake Hart's hand. 'Real good to see you again, John. How was the flight?'

'Fine, fine. It's one of those flights where you only just have time to get used to being in the air before you start to come down again.'

'I guess if you're used to flying the North Atlantic this just seems like a short hop. Sit down, sit down, I'll get Mary to bring us some coffee. How do you take yours?'

The coffee came, and Connors sat down behind his oak desk, a massive piece of furniture which looked somewhat out of place in front of the floor to ceiling window. 'We've got about 20 minutes before the meeting convenes. Anything you need to talk over before it starts?'

'No, I don't think so. You've seen the draft I sent you; what do you think?'

'Well, I have shown it to my colleagues, but we have not had a chance so far to discuss it, and I think it would be a little premature of me to comment one way or the other before we've had a full discussion. I will say that you've made a good job of this so far, and this fellow Macallister seems to be worth his fee. I'd like to meet him.'

'I'll try and arrange for him to come down from Montreal some time when you come up to see us. I assume that if this goes ahead, you will be coming up to make sure we really know what we're talking about.'

Connors laughed. 'I think you can count on it. How's that wife of yours? She's in some kind of business as well, isn't she?'

'Yes, she owns her own company.' He talked for a while about Wendy, wondering as he did so what he could ever have found objectionable about what she was doing. Then, suddenly, the time was up, and Connors was saying, 'We'd better make a move. Don't want to keep the others waiting.'

Unsurprisingly the Laurentian boardroom was considerably larger and grander than Wentworth's. The long table was so highly polished that you could see the sky's reflection in its surface. Following Connors into the room, Hart was greeted by those directors he knew and introduced to those he didn't; there were a few minutes of casual conversation during which, he knew, they were sizing him up. Then Connors called the meeting to order, and Hart sat where he was directed, about halfway down the left side of the table.

Apart from a few administrative matters there was only one item on the agenda: the strategic review completed by Wentworth Mouldings of Hamilton, Ontario. He sat silently while Connors outlined Wentworth's current position and explained how Hart had been appointed CEO the previous summer, and gave a brief but pointedly accurate precis of Hart's own background. The others around the table were looking at their copies of his strategic review document while they listened. Then Connors said, 'Now I'm going to turn it over to the man himself. John, maybe you'd like to tell us a little bit about this document and explain what it is you want from us.'

'Thank you, Mike.' He leaned forward, clearing his throat as ten pair of eyes turned to look at him. 'Well, you all appear to have seen the document, and I presume you've had a chance to read through it. It contains details specific to our company and our present situation; I won't go into all those details here and now, although I'm quite prepared to answer individual questions about them if you wish. But I feel the details, even the details about the levels of funding and investment that we require, are of secondary importance. What is most important is the rationale behind our decisions at this point, and if you understand and agree with that rationale, then I think the details will fall into place. What I want to explain here is not so much what we're doing, but why we're doing it.'

He saw Connors nod; an encouraging sign.

Hart then quickly sketched in the background to where Wentworth's request for investment was turned down.

'Now, that refusal,' explained Hart, 'was probably the best thing you could have done for us, because it really focused our minds.' There were one or two smiles around the table, but Connors' face was perfectly serious. 'Previous to this point, we had all assumed that it was all quite simple; growth was good and not growing was bad. Like most of our competitors, we took orders from anybody, particularly existing customers or in sectors where we were already present. Our main aim was to grow as fast as possible, somewhat regardless of direction. But when we looked at the issue more closely, we began to wonder if that really was the answer. And, with that vague idea in mind, we set to work.'

Hart then spent the next hour detailing how the proposal before them had been developed while clarifying points as they arose. He carefully drew out key distinctions and analyses concerning segmentation, volumes, contribution levels and options for coping with market differences. As the presentation progressed, Hart found how well the logic fitted together.

'So, there it is,' he concluded. 'You've seen what we propose to do, and I hope I've adequately explained the background issues and concepts involved. As far as future investment is concerned, we have set goals for each of the three business units, and we want associated levels of investment to meet those different goals. This increased investment, coupled with the increased profitability of the business following this restructuring, should make Wentworth a successful company for some years to come.'

That was that. He stopped, suddenly thinking of all the other things he should have said, all the details he should have explained. There was a silence that lasted for several seconds before Mike Connors raised his head and said, 'Thanks, John, I'm sure we all found that very helpful. Well? Anybody have any questions they want to ask?'

The man across the table from Hart, a senior finance executive, said, 'I did read your appendix giving key analyses with considerable interest. But I'm a little concerned by some apparent omissions. For instance, while you have stated the size of your "new" markets, I am unable to find the detail from which these figures are taken.'

Hart sat for a moment, suddenly wondering how best to restate what he had just presented. 'In overall terms, we have put to one side our traditional view of markets. However, this approach has obvious advantages in terms of expressing overall size and our current and projected market shares. Our market sales revenue figures draw business from several traditional sectors and this detail, as you rightly point out, is not included here. However, I have copies of this information with me and I was intending to leave them with you so that you can review the data at a later time. What we have assessed is that the market served by each unit is of an order of magnitude greater than either our current or future capacity could support. Identifying markets in terms of their order-winners and developing a manufacturing strategy to support these is the platform we wish to establish in order to grow both sales revenue and profits. Orienting our marketing and sales efforts to attract business consistent with the focus of one or more units is part of the strategic approach. Our job now is to stay on our toes in order to anticipate possible changes.'

'Do you mean to say you've no idea what your markets will do next year?'

'Of course we know what they will do in general. We stay in touch through our marketing and sales staff, and we know what the likely trends are. Again, you will see the projected sales in the appendix to the report you have in front of you with supporting detail.'

'It sounds very pat,' said another director. 'One big plant can't do the job, but three little ones can? You're still going to have the same throughput and the same production capacity. This just sounds like you're repackaging the old plant.'

'But we won't have the same production capacity,' Hart said. 'We have assumed all along that we will have to increase capacity, and we want to do so now more than ever. The difference is that we want to increase capacity in selected areas, where it is necessary, rather than across the board. In this way we will improve our plant according to actual needs rather than on a more general basis, and the Group will be more likely to see a good return on its investment. Believe me, if you read through the structural and infrastructural changes we are proposing, you will see that this is not repackaging.'

'No, I can see that,' said a third. 'My worry is more in the opposite direction. I quite understand the rationale for breaking up the manufacturing plant into focused units, that seems sensible and I think it probably will give you the result you are seeking. But why split up the infrastructure as well? Is that really necessary? And what is the impact on overhead costs?'

'As you can imagine, we've gone over the numbers time and time again,' Hart said, 'and we are positive that in the end the increased profits will more than match the increased costs. For example, when you buy a computer, you don't buy an expensive machine and then run it with second-rate software. On the contrary, you buy the best available, the best meaning that which is best suited to the tasks which will be demanded of it. That's what we're doing with the infrastructure which surrounds manufacturing. As manufacturing changes, infrastructure has to change to support it.'

'And can't a centralised plant do that?'

'Will it do it as well? We looked at that question and decided it would not. You see, we also want to focus people's minds as well as the actual physical side of the plant. We want to not only be able to be flexible in meeting customers' needs, but be much more aggressive than we presently are about going out and getting business according to our needs. But these infrastructure changes have been done within the provisos I mentioned earlier. Accounting and finance, as well as personnel, serve as examples. And we debated long and hard what to do about marketing and decided in the end to retain a centralised marketing and sales division although certain members of the marketing department will have responsibility for certain business units. We decided that we couldn't expect our customers to deal with three different marketing departments depending on the type of order they want to place.'

'So do you envision these business units competing with one another?'

Hart drew a deep breath. 'No,' he said. 'My job, as CEO, and that of my fellow directors, is going to be to see that they do not compete with one another, and that they keep their eyes firmly fixed on the goals we at the top have set for them. That, I grant you, is going to be hard work. We have business targets, and everybody has targets of their own. There is no incentive for anyone to go off on their own; everything revolves around meeting those goals. And, of course, the goals themselves are under constant review as we monitor changes in markets, customers and products.'

'It looks good on paper,' said a fourth director. 'Can you make it work in practice?'

'Yes,' Hart said simply. 'I've got a good team and reliable support from the independent consultant I mentioned earlier. My staff are all highly enthusiastic about the idea and looking forward to putting it into practice. We have both the skill and the will.'

Up at the head of the table Mike Connors nodded suddenly and made a marginal note on his copy of the proposal. Other questions followed; these were more detailed, searching through the figures Alan Mills had put together and querying various items of investment. Before he left Wentworth the four of them had discussed whether or not to be flexible on some of these points and had decided in the end to be resolute; stand up for everything, Mills had advised, and if in the end they decided to cut something out, that's their prerogative. Everything that's in this document is there for a reason.

They queried his reasons for supporting growth targets. The new reorganisation was assigning a disproportionate share of future capacity to the mid-volume, high-quality unit. They asked him how he had arrived at those figures, and the question of market size came up again; he explained, with more patience this time, that these figures represented the maximisation of profits. If volumes increased much beyond these targets, a further reorganisation may then become necessary.

It all took much longer than he expected. It was over two hours later when Connors, who had said very little throughout the meeting, dropped his pencil and leaned back in his chair and said, 'Well, I think we've been around the houses, and I don't think there's anything new we can discuss. John, we're going to have to throw you out about now and have our discussion. I'll get Mary to take you back to my office and give you a cup of coffee. If you prefer, there's a bottle of bourbon in my desk drawer; that is, if we've taken too much out of you.'

Hart laughed with the others and got to his feet. 'I haven't lost that much blood. Thank you all, gentlemen.'

Back in Connors' office he sat on the sofa for a few minutes with his cup of coffee, staring into the cup and reflecting that if the world coffee industry were ever to collapse, most of the rest of the international business community would probably feel the impact through lack of sustenance. After a few minutes the tension became too much and he got up and walked across to the big window, looking down at the street 15 floors below his feet.

Now was the time to try to think what he would say and do if the men in the boardroom said no. If he had the courage of his convictions, he would resign and try and find another job. But that was not as easy as it sounded. And besides, would quitting really help anyone? Wouldn't it look like he was going off in a sulk, instead of tackling the problem head on?

It would not be the end of the world. There were still things which could be done. A partial reorganisation of the plant along the lines they had been describing could still be effected; there would be cost savings there, at least in the short term. The marketing plan, too, could be re-focused on the three target markets, and while they wouldn't get the whole effect, they might at least get some of it. The company would not grow, of course, and capacity would not increase and there would still be problems of trying to squeeze new business into crowded production schedules, but, again in the short term, they could lift profits some. Enough, perhaps, to prove to Laurentian that they had been right.

And there was another benefit, of course, which was already evident. The managers and staff of Wentworth were already thinking more like a team. Nick Moretti was actively looking for the links between marketing's job and his own. Shirley Easton was convinced that manufacturing had to push marketing just as much as marketing had to pull manufacturing. Alan Mills was going out and searching for ways of making more profits, rather than pulling in the reins and worrying solely about costs. And that same enthusiasm was seeping down through the managers and even into the sales staff and the shop floor. There had already been, in the last few months, a seismic shift in attitudes in the company, and that was something that could not be rolled back.

But. . . . If time went by and the gains which had been promised did not materialise, wouldn't people get disillusioned? It's easy to talk about theoretical change and admire its benefits, but at some point change has got to be realised. That was a point which Wendy had recognised before he had. Change requires momentum, and once the pace of change slows it becomes harder to pick it up again.

That was his great fear; that the enthusiasm and impetus which had been built up over the last few minutes would dissipate with nothing to show for it. He did not like the thought of returning to the old days, and in fact, it would be worse than the old days. Some of the people who had worked so long on these ideas would go somewhere else where there was a chance of putting them into practice. Shirley Easton was one. Strategy isn't imposed from on high, it is enacted throughout, at every level.

Now more than ever, Hart appreciated the truth of the old saying: adapt or die. There is no middle ground between growth and stagnation.

Behind him the door opened and Mike Connors came into the office, saying something over his shoulder to Mary. Hart glanced at his watch and was surprised to see that 30 minutes had passed.

'Better have a seat,' Connors said. 'I always hate to see people stand too close to that window. It's a long way down.'

Hart looked once more at the tiny people and vehicles crawling along below him, and then went back to his chair.

'Right,' said Connors, a bit more briskly than usual. 'I thought you handled that very well, John. They didn't always agree with what you said, but they respected your answers, and that's usually just as good. After you were gone, we thrashed it all out again, as you might have expected. Jim Ahrenson, the guy who was quizzing you so closely at the start, says he thinks it looks good on paper, but you'll never do it. He raises, rightly, all sorts of potential problems of implementation which you haven't discussed. There are several queries about whether your cost figures for expansion are indeed realistic, and if they're not, of course, then your profit forecasts are going to be thrown out of whack as well.'

Hart said nothing. Connors was not asking questions; he was summing up a case, much as a judge might do. 'There were also the inevitable queries about your consultant friend,' Connors went on, 'and whether he knows what he is talking about. Fortunately Alex Murray and one or two of the others had read some of his articles and books and had good things to say. And there were queries too about control. A lot of it comes down to you yourself, John, and in the end we've had to pass judgement on whether you personally could deliver on your promises.

'The biggest single problem is whether or nor these changes can be implemented as you say they can. You'll have to forgive us if we want evidence as we go along. We're proposing, therefore, that any investment be provided in stages, linked to phased implementation, and that we have the right of full review of each phase before deciding whether to grant the next stage of investment. Can you live with that?'

Hart looked up. It suddenly dawned on him what was on offer. 'And in return, you'll give us the full package we've asked for?'

'Every last penny of it.' Connors grinned and held out his hand.

CONCLUSION

The morning sun was shining brightly through the office windows. Hart put his briefcase down on the desk and poured himself a cup of coffee. It was done. He had taken the ideas to Philadelphia, and sold them. He had secured approval from the board to re-organise and expand the company, and he had won the promise for the necessary funds in full. In a world where good ideas rarely got beyond the talking stage, he had a chance to turn his ideas into reality.

He took a sip of his coffee, looking out across the yard. He smiled, a little wryly, for he was under no illusions about his position. Selling the ideas had been only the first step. The hard work was about to begin. They now had to be implemented. . . .

Other business books by Terry Hill

- **Small Business: Production/Operations Management;** Macmillan (1987), Basingstoke, UK

- **The Essence of Operations Management;** Prentice Hall International (1993), Hemel Hempstead, UK

- **Manufacturing Strategy: The Strategic Management of the Manufacturing Function;** Macmillan 2nd ed (1993), Basingstoke, UK

- **Manufacturing Strategy: Text and Cases;** Irwin 2nd edition (1994), Burr Ridge, Illinois, USA (USA and Canada only)

- **Manufacturing Strategy: Text and Cases;** Macmillan (1995), Basingstoke, UK, World rights (excluding USA and Canada)